The Weekend Cook

The Weekend Cook

SPEND YOUR WEEKEND ON
A GASTRONOMIC ADVENTURE

This edition published by Parragon Books Ltd in 2015 and distributed by

Parragon Inc.
440 Park Avenue South, 13th Floor
New York, NY 10016
www.parragon.com/lovefood

LOVE FOOD is an imprint of Parragon Books Ltd

ISBN 978-1-4723-9259-6

Printed in China

Introduction and extra text written by Anne Sheasby
Cover photography by Haarala Hamilton

Notes for the Reader
This book uses standard kitchen measuring spoons and cups. All spoon and cup measurements
are level unless otherwise indicated. Unless otherwise stated, milk is assumed to be whole,
eggs are large, individual vegetables are medium, and pepper is freshly ground black
pepper. Unless otherwise stated, all root vegetables should be peeled prior to using.

The times given are only an approximate guide. Preparation times differ according to the
techniques used by different people and the cooking times may also vary from those given.

Contents

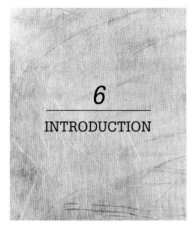

Introduction

Weekends are important, so make yours count by turning mealtimes into edible adventures. Shake off the week and kick back with a selection of mind-blowing recipes that will transform your cooking repertoire from mundane to magic. Make the most of everyday ingredients and look forward to eating meals you'll never forget.

This inspiring book is perfect for cooks who look forward to spending the weekend getting creative in the kitchen and experimenting with exciting new flavors. Whether you are planning a Friday night in with your version of a takeout, or are inviting people over for a decadent dinner party, it's the only cookbook you'll need when the weekend arrives.

We'll take you on a culinary journey through the weekend, tempting you along the way with a fantastic choice of dishes, some relatively straightforward and others more challenging. There is something to suit all the more adventurous cooks out there and those who enjoy venturing farther afield to hunt out unusual ingredients and create impressive dishes that demand a little more time. This book is for visionary cooks who enjoy experimenting and want to create lasting food memories.

Friday night is the beginning of the weekend wind-down, so we start with a sizzling selection of tempting takeout-style dishes from all over the world that are sure to get the weekend off to a great start. Instead of reaching for the usual takeout menu, why not spend a little time rustling up one of these awesome options that will put your Friday-night menu on the food map?

Then, to kick things off on a Saturday, we include a savvy selection of breakfasts and lunches to set you up perfectly for whatever the day has in store. This section features a variety of options, from power-packed recipes to sustain your weekend energy to nutty mini muffins and a choice of wonderful bagels, sandwiches, and wraps. For those fitness fans who enjoy a Saturday morning workout, we also include a couple of power-packed beverages to give you a boost before you start.

A chapter on Saturday evening specials covers all things extravagant, and encourages the adventurous cook in you to go the extra mile and create some amazing meals to share. This incredible selection of impressive, lavish main dishes and to-die-for desserts is sure to result in an onslaught of compliments from your hugely impressed guests. Plus, you'll relish the opportunity to push the boat out and experiment with new ideas every weekend.

Next up, we feature some great brunch dishes that are perfect for a relaxed Sunday morning, such as eggs, pancakes, frittatas, tarts, platters, and even a few perky cocktails. With these recipes, you can show off your flair for creating the all-time best brunches that will have your friends lining up outside your door, eager to sample your culinary skills and enjoy the chance to chill out over some delicious dishes.

Get set to impress on a Sunday with one of our long and lazy lunches, ideal for taking your time over. We feature a selection of sweet and not-so-sweet options, including classic roasts as well as slow-cooked meals, plus tempting desserts to satisfy any sweet cravings.

For all budding bakers out there, the next chapter on breads for the weekend is ideal for you. It's hard to resist the unmistakable aroma of freshly baked bread, so now you can try your hand at creating some bistro-style breads to serve to your guests.

We even include a final chapter encompassing a few recipes to boost your mood, and your energy levels, and to make sure your Monday morning kicks off with a blast, including rejuvenating juices, energy cookies, and power snacks.

So, if you're a food fanatic who relishes spending time experimenting with recipes and ingredients, creating food you love to eat, then you'll enjoy this culinary journey through a sensational selection of mind-blowing dishes.

Hints & Tips for Weekend Cooking

On Saturday morning, make some time to visit your local farmers' market to see what culinary treats and interesting foods are available. Farmers' markets are typically home to a wide variety of high-quality producers of delicious food and beverages, giving you the opportunity to buy local produce direct from the supplier. You can wander around savoring the aromas and flavors from the samples offered, and try out some mouthwatering new ingredients in readiness for creating some tasty meals for the weekend.

It's also worth checking nearby farm stores and local speciality or artisan food suppliers. It's amazing to discover the wide range of foods on your doorstep, so make good use of these food fanatics in your region. In season, pick-your-own farms offer plentiful supplies of fresh fruit and vegetables, providing fresh produce and plenty of inspiration for weekend cooking.

All year round, local fruit and vegetable markets offer seasonal produce as well as some more unusual things to try. Local butchers and fish dealers are worth a visit if you are looking for something specific or simply wanting to find some inspiration. They can offer valuable advice on suitable cooking techniques and recipes for the various cuts of meat or fish, be it a simple idea or a more adventurous one. Artisan bakers, too, are good for baking inspiration and ideas, or if you just want a great-tasting loaf of bread or rolls to accompany lunch. They often stock fresh yeast, too. Many supermarkets also have trained experts on hand who can offer you tips of their trade.

Speciality food markets, fairs, and festivals are great places to visit and discover new food trends and ingredients. The variety of products available, as well as all the enticing aromas wafting around, will provide a truly awesome assault on your senses.

If you are lucky enough to live near Asian, Greek, Italian, Mexican, Polish, or other speciality supermarkets, food stores, or delis, take a look at the amazing array of fresh, dried, frozen, and pantry items they have to offer—the wide choice will provide you with endless opportunities to get experimenting in the kitchen. Taste any samples available and choose something that you perhaps haven't thought of trying before.

Try to be organized and have some idea of what meals you are planning before you venture out to do the shopping. However, do allow for some flexibility when selecting ingredients, too, in case a new or interesting ingredient sparks a slightly different idea or direction to go in.

Be bold and courageous and try your hand at new cooking techniques. Every couple of weekends or so, why not set yourself a target or challenge to try a new skill and add to your ever-increasing repertoire of recipes? Aim to challenge yourself without overstretching your skills.

The weekend is also the ideal time for experimenting with new kitchen gadgets, appliances, and accessories that you have recently bought. Take the time to get familiar with the appliance and see what culinary wonders you can create with its help.

It's a good idea to plan and manage your time in the kitchen, so you have plenty of scope for preparing and cooking your meal, as well as enough time for experimenting and enjoying the whole process as well. Allow some time for trying out something new, plus ample time to relax and kick back along the way as well. Prepare things in advance where possible so you have more time to spend with friends, or get your guests involved with the cooking, so you can enjoy their company over a few beers as you cook together.

Above all, use this wonderful book to showcase your skills, flaunt your flair, and impress your guests with your competent and creative cooking.

Friday Night

Global Takeout

It's Friday night and, after a frantic week at work, it's time to wind down, chill out, and enjoy a casual Friday night dinner. Once you head home from work, making the most of a relaxed evening in will be top of the list, so a homemade version of a classic takeout will hit the spot and satisfy any hunger pangs. Most of these recipes can be thrown together fairly easily, and any fresh ingredients that you'll need can be picked up at the supermarket or local deli or store on your way home from work.

Friday night is the perfect time to chill out with a group of friends or spend a quiet evening in, so whatever the occasion or company, we include a tempting collection of popular takeout dishes from around the globe, from burgers and pizzas to kabobs and curries.

You can also create some simple accompaniments that can be whipped up easily and without too much effort to serve alongside these recipes. They include fresh crusty bread, steamed rice, baked potato wedges, or naan, winter or summer slaw, a mixed leaf or seasonal salad tossed in a zingy dressing, as well as one or two of your finest homemade chutneys, pickles, salsas, or flavored mustard or mayo. Or for something a little different, check the sauce recipes for inspiration, such as Chipotle Ketchup or Chipotle Mustard.

We've got it all covered, so why not start by inviting your friends around and impressing them with an all-time favorite, such as Cheeseburgers with Fries or Beer-Battered Fish with Fries? Side orders of ketchup and mustard are all you'll need to complete the meal.

If an impromptu or casual dinner party is more your thing for a Friday night, try tempting guests to the table with flavorful dishes from afar, including Chicken Chow Mein from China, Pork Pad Thai from Thailand, or Chipotle Pork Fajitas from Mexico.

For big appetites and those who favor some extra heat and spice in their food, recipes such as Colossal Lamb Kabob with Hot Chili Sauce or Blazing Hot Wings with Blue Cheese Dressing are guaranteed to hit the spicy spot.

On the other hand, if you decide to opt for a fun Friday movie night, sophisticated snacks, including Rosemary, Sea Salt & Sesame Popcorn, or Root Vegetable Chips, are sure to tantalize the taste buds.

So, whatever the occasion, or the company you are in, this chapter features something delicious for everyone to enjoy. Check our feature on savvy pantry spices, too, where we offer on-trend tips for how to add maximum flavor to dishes to create tasty meals after work.

So, as the working week draws to a close and Friday night marks the beginning of a great weekend ahead, all you have to do is to decide on your food mood, select the recipe of your choice, pour yourself a glass of something chilled, put your favorite background music on, and let the creative cooking begin.

Cheeseburgers with Fries

The secret to making top-notch fries is to double-fry them. Take the time to make these delicious homemade fries and you'll appreciate the extra effort when you enjoy them alongside the succulent grilled cheeseburgers.

SERVES 4
Prepares in 30–35 minutes,
  plus soaking and cooling

Cheeseburgers

1½ pounds freshly ground beef chuck

1 beef bouillon cube

1 tablespoon minced dried onion

2 tablespoons water

1–2 tablespoons sunflower oil

½ cup shredded cheddar, Swiss, or
  American cheese

lettuce leaves

4 hamburger buns, halved

tomato slices

Fries

6 russet potatoes (about 1½ pounds)

sunflower, vegetable, or peanut oil,
  for deep-frying

salt and pepper

1. To make the cheeseburgers, put the ground beef into a large mixing bowl. Crumble the bouillon cube over the beef, add the dried onion and water, and mix well with a metal spoon to combine.

2. Divide the meat into four portions, shape each into a ball, then flatten slightly to make a patty of your preferred thickness.

3. Place a ridged grill pan over medium–high heat. Lightly brush the patties with oil and cook for 5–6 minutes. Turn the patties, sprinkle the cheese over the cooked side, and cook for an additional 5–6 minutes, or until cooked to your preference. Set aside and keep warm.

4. To make the fries, peel the potatoes and cut into even ⅜-inch-thick sticks. As soon as they have been prepared, put the potatoes into a large bowl of cold water to prevent discoloration, then let them soak for 30 minutes to remove the excess starch.

5. Drain the potatoes and dry thoroughly on a clean dish towel. Preheat the oil in a deep fryer or large, heavy saucepan to 375°F. If you do not have a thermometer, test the temperature by dropping a potato stick into the oil. If it sinks, the oil isn't hot enough; if it floats and the oil bubbles around the potato, it is ready.

6. Carefully add a small batch of potatoes to the oil (this is to be sure of even cooking and to avoid reducing the temperature of the oil) and deep-fry for 5–6 minutes, or until softened but not browned. Remove from the oil and drain well on paper towels.

7. Let the fries cool for at least 5 minutes. Continue to deep-fry the remaining potatoes in the same way, letting the oil return to the correct temperature each time.

8. When ready to serve the fries, reheat the oil to 400°F. Add the potatoes, in small batches, and deep-fry for 2–3 minutes, until golden brown. Remove from the oil and drain on paper towels.

9. To serve, place the lettuce leaves on the bottom halves of the hamburger buns and top with the cheeseburgers. Place a couple of tomato slices on top of the burger and add the bun lids. Season the fries to taste with salt and pepper, then serve alongside the burgers.

Beer-Battered Fish with Fries

The bubbles in the beer add body and lightness to this supercrispy batter that encases the moist and succulent fish fillets inside. Served with hand-cut fries and mashed peas, this will be a popular dish among family and friends alike.

SERVES 4
Prepares in 30 minutes,
 plus chilling and soaking
Cooks in 35–40 minutes

vegetable oil, for deep-frying
6 russet potatoes (about 1½ pounds),
 prepared as described on page 17
4 thick cod fillets, about 6 ounces each
salt and pepper
lemon wedges, to serve

Batter
1¾ cups all-purpose flour,
 plus extra for dusting
1¾ teaspoons baking powder
½ teaspoon salt
1¼ cups cold beer

Mashed Peas
2⅓ cups frozen peas
2 tablespoons butter
2 tablespoons light cream
salt and pepper

1. For the batter, sift the flour and baking powder into a bowl with the salt and whisk in most of the beer. Add the remaining beer; it should be thick, like heavy cream. Chill in the refrigerator for half an hour.

2. To make the peas, cook them in lightly salted boiling water for 3 minutes. Drain and mash to a thick puree, add the butter and cream, and season to taste. Set aside and keep warm.

3. Heat the oil to 50°F in a deep fryer or a large, heavy saucepan. Preheat the oven to 300°F. Fry the potatoes for 8–10 minutes, or until softened but not browned. Drain on paper towels and put into a dish in the oven. Increase the temperature of the oil to 350°F.

4. Season the fish to taste and dust lightly with flour. Dip one fillet in the batter and coat thickly. Carefully place in the hot oil and repeat with the other fillets. Cook for 8–10 minutes, turning over halfway through. Drain and keep warm.

5. Reheat the oil to 350°F and recook the fries for 2–3 minutes, or until golden brown and cooked through. Drain and season to taste. Serve the fries with the fish, peas, and lemon wedges for squeezing over the fish.

Margherita Pizza

Make the dough for this tasty pizza as soon as you get home from work and let it rise as you wind down. Then get to work on the topping and you'll soon be serving the perfect Friday night pizza!

SERVES 2
Prepares in 40 minutes, plus rising
Cooks in 40–50 minutes

1 tablespoon butter
1 tablespoon olive oil, plus extra for brushing and drizzling
1 small onion, finely chopped
1 garlic clove, finely chopped
½ celery stalk, finely chopped
¾ cup canned diced tomatoes
1 tablespoon tomato paste
light brown sugar, to taste
1 tablespoon chopped fresh basil
3 tablespoons water
5 ounces mozzarella cheese, sliced
4 tomatoes, sliced
1 fresh basil sprig
2 tablespoons grated Parmesan cheese
salt and pepper

Pizza Dough

1⅔ cups white bread flour, plus extra for dusting
1 teaspoon salt
½ teaspoon active dry yeast
1 tablespoon olive oil, plus extra for oiling
⅔ cup lukewarm water

1. To make the dough, sift the flour and salt into a bowl and stir in the yeast. Make a well in the center and pour in the oil and water, then mix to a soft dough. Knead for 10 minutes on a lightly floured surface. Shape into a ball, place in an oiled plastic bag, and let rise in a warm place for 1 hour, or until doubled.

2. Melt the butter with the oil in a saucepan. Add the onion, garlic, and celery and cook over low heat, stirring occasionally, for 5 minutes, until softened. Stir in the canned tomatoes, tomato paste, sugar to taste, chopped basil, and water, then season to taste with salt and pepper. Increase the heat to medium and bring to a boil, then reduce the heat and simmer, stirring occasionally, for 15–20 minutes, or until thickened. Remove from the heat and set aside.

3. Preheat the oven to 425°F. Brush a baking sheet with oil. Punch down the dough and knead briefly on a lightly floured surface. Roll out into a circle and transfer to the prepared baking sheet. Push up a rim all the way around.

4. Spread the tomato sauce evenly over the crust. Arrange the mozzarella and tomato slices alternately on top. Coarsely tear the basil leaves and put them on the pizza, then sprinkle with the Parmesan. Drizzle with the oil and bake in the preheated oven for 15–20 minutes, or until crisp and golden. Serve the pizza immediately.

Lamb-Cumin Pita Burgers with Tahini Sauce

Lightly toast, then grind, whole cumin seeds to add the finest spice flavor to these tempting lamb burgers, and use individual round pita breads instead of halving larger oval ones, for extra appeal, too.

SERVES 6
Prepares in 20–25 minutes
Cooks in 10–14 minutes

1 pound fresh ground lamb
3 tablespoons finely chopped red onion
1 tablespoon chopped fresh cilantro, plus extra leaves to garnish
1 teaspoon salt
½ teaspoon pepper
½ teaspoon ground cumin
3 large pita breads, warmed, halved, and sliced
tomato slices
cucumber slices
olive oil, for drizzling
salt and pepper

Tahini Sauce
⅓ cup tahini
⅓ cup plain yogurt
1 garlic clove, finely chopped

1. Preheat the broiler to high. Put the lamb into a bowl and add the onion, cilantro, salt, pepper, and cumin, then gently mix until thoroughly combined.

2. Divide the mixture into six equal portions, form each portion into a 3-inch wide patty, and place in a broiler pan lined with aluminum foil.

3. Put the broiler pan under the preheated broiler and cook the patties for 5–7 minutes on each side, or until cooked through and browned.

4. To make the tahini sauce, put the tahini, yogurt, and garlic into a bowl. Season to taste with salt and pepper and mix to combine.

5. Stuff the burgers into the pita halves, then drizzle with the tahini sauce. Add the tomato and cucumber slices and the cilantro leaves, drizzle with the oil, and serve immediately.

Chicken Chow Mein

Transport your taste buds to China and create this popular takeout dish in the comfort of your own kitchen. Taking just a matter of minutes to prepare and cook, it's the ideal fodder for a Friday night.

SERVES 4
Prepares in 15 minutes
Cooks in 17 minutes

8 ounces dried medium
  Chinese egg noodles
2 tablespoons sunflower oil
2 cups shredded, cooked chicken breasts
1 garlic clove, finely chopped
1 red bell pepper, thinly sliced
3½ ounces shiitake mushrooms, sliced
6 scallions, sliced
1 cup bean sprouts
3 tablespoons soy sauce
1 tablespoon sesame oil

1. Cook the noodles according to the package directions. Drain well and set aside.

2. Heat a wok over medium heat, then add the oil. Add the shredded chicken, garlic, red bell pepper, mushrooms, scallions, and bean sprouts to the wok and stir-fry for about 5 minutes.

3. Add the noodles to the wok, toss well, and stir-fry for an additional 5 minutes. Drizzle with the soy sauce and sesame oil and toss until thoroughly combined. Transfer to warm bowls and serve immediately.

Thai Green Chicken Curry & Udon Noodles

Rustled up in less than an hour, this truly authentic Thai green curry is bursting with fresh flavors and vibrant green herbs. Serve with a refreshingly crisp cucumber salad for a truly tasty meal.

SERVES 4
Prepares in 20–25 minutes,
 plus cooling
Cooks in 25–28 minutes

1 tablespoon vegetable oil
1 shallot, diced
1–3 teaspoons Thai green curry paste
1 (14-ounce) can coconut milk
1 tablespoon Thai fish sauce
juice of 1 lime
1 tablespoon packed light brown sugar
½ cup fresh basil leaves
¼ cup fresh cilantro leaves
1 pound fresh udon noodles
2½ cups shredded cooked chicken
3 scallions, thinly sliced,
 to garnish

1. Heat the oil in a nonstick skillet over medium heat. Add the shallot and cook for 5 minutes, until soft. Add the curry paste and cook, stirring, for 1 minute.

2. Open the can of coconut milk and scoop off the thick cream that will have risen to the top. Add the coconut cream to the pan with the fish sauce, lime juice, and sugar. Cook, stirring frequently, for 1–2 minutes.

3. Stir in the remaining coconut milk and bring the mixture to a boil. Reduce the heat to low and simmer, stirring occasionally, for an additional 5 minutes, or until the sauce thickens. Remove from the heat and let cool slightly.

4. Transfer the mixture to a food processor, add the basil and cilantro, and process until smooth and bright green. Return the sauce to the pan and reheat over medium–low heat.

5. Cook the noodles according to the package directions and put them into a large serving bowl.

6. Add the chicken and sauce to the noodles and toss to combine. Serve immediately, garnished with the scallions.

Bengali Vegetable Curry

An aromatic mixed vegetable curry, served simply with some perfect fluffy rice, creates this standout vegetarian dish that is ideal for enjoying at the end of a busy working week.

SERVES 2
Prepares in 20–25 minutes,
 plus soaking
Cooks in 28–35 minutes

⅓ cup white poppy seeds
3 tablespoons black mustard seeds
2 teaspoons grated fresh ginger
¼ cup vegetable or peanut oil
2 green chiles, split lengthwise
1 tablespoon Chinese five-spice powder
2 cups ½-inch fresh bitter melon (karela)
 or squash cubes
2 Yukon gold or red-skinned potatoes,
 cut into ½-inch cubes
1 eggplant, cut into ½-inch cubes
1 zucchini, cut into ½-inch cubes
1 carrot, cut into ½-inch cubes
1 tomato, finely chopped
⅔ cup fresh or frozen peas
1¾ cups cold water
¼ teaspoon ground turmeric
2 teaspoons salt
1 teaspoon palm or brown sugar
½ cup milk

1. Soak the white poppy seeds and 2 tablespoons of the mustard seeds in a bowl of warm water for 1 hour. Drain the seeds and blend well with the ginger to make a paste.

2. Heat the oil in a large skillet and add the remaining mustard seeds and the chiles. When the mustard seeds start to pop, add the five-spice powder and all the vegetables. Add half of the water and stir to mix well, then cover tightly and cook, stirring frequently, over medium heat for 10–12 minutes.

3. Add half of the white poppy seed-and-mustard seed paste, the turmeric, and salt. Add the remaining water and cook, stirring frequently, over low–medium heat for an additional 10–15 minutes.

4. Add the remaining white poppy seed-and-mustard seed paste, the palm sugar, and milk and cook for an additional 5 minutes, or until the vegetables are tender. Remove the chillies and serve immediately.

Pork Pad Thai

This popular Thai pork noodle dish is quick and easy to create at home, making it the ideal choice for a Friday night dinner with friends. A wonderful fusion of fresh flavors, it's sure to impress your guests.

SERVES 4
Prepares in 20 minutes
Cooks in 15–20 minutes

8 ounces thick dried rice noodles
2 tablespoons peanut or vegetable oil
4 scallions, coarsely chopped
2 garlic cloves, crushed
2 red chiles, seeded and sliced
8 ounces pork tenderloin, trimmed
  and thinly sliced
4 ounces cooked peeled large shrimp
juice of 1 lime
2 tablespoons Thai fish sauce
2 eggs, beaten
½ cup fresh bean sprouts
handful of chopped fresh cilantro
⅓ cup chopped unsalted peanuts
lime wedges, to serve (optional)

1. Prepare the noodles according to the package directions. Drain and set aside.

2. Heat a wok over medium–high heat, then add the oil. Add the scallions, garlic, and chiles and stir-fry for 1–2 minutes. Add the pork and stir-fry over high heat for 1–2 minutes, or until the pork is completely cooked through.

3. Add the shrimp, lime juice, fish sauce, and eggs and stir-fry over medium heat for 2–3 minutes, until the eggs have set and the shrimp are heated through.

4. Add the bean sprouts, most of the cilantro, the peanuts, and the noodles and stir-fry for 30 seconds until heated through. Garnish with the remaining cilantro and serve immediately with lime wedges, if desired.

Hot & Spicy Ketchup

MAKES ABOUT 2½ CUPS
Prepares in 15 minutes
Cooks in 2½ hours

5 pounds tomatoes, chopped

2 red jalapeño chiles, chopped

1 sweet white onion,
coarsely chopped

1 teaspoon salt, plus extra to taste

1 teaspoon fennel seeds

1 teaspoon black mustard seeds

1 cup apple cider vinegar

½ cup firmly packed
light brown sugar

1 cinnamon stick

½ teaspoon ground nutmeg

½ teaspoon sweet paprika

1–3 teaspoons cayenne pepper

pepper

1. Put the tomatoes, chiles, onion, and salt into a large saucepan over high heat. Stir until the tomatoes begin to break down, then reduce the heat to low, cover, and simmer for 30 minutes, or until the tomatoes are pulpy.

2. Meanwhile, put the fennel seeds and mustard seeds on a square of cheesecloth, bring together the sides, and tie to make a bag, then set aside.

3. Pass the tomato mixture through a strainer into a large saucepan, rubbing back and forth with a wooden spoon and scraping the bottom of the strainer to produce as much puree as possible.

4. Add the spice bag and the vinegar, sugar, cinnamon stick, nutmeg, paprika, and cayenne pepper. Season to taste with pepper, then stir until the sugar dissolves. Bring to a boil, then reduce the heat and simmer, uncovered, for 1½ hours, skimming the surface as necessary, until the sauce is reduced and thickened.

5. Remove the spice bag and the cinnamon stick. Transfer to a bowl and let cool completely.

6. The ketchup can be used immediately, or stored in an airtight container in the refrigerator for up to 1 month.

Sweet Chili Sauce

MAKES ABOUT ⅔ CUP
Prepares in 15 minutes
Cooks in 25 minutes

4 red jalapeño chiles, halved

*2 large garlic cloves,
coarsely chopped*

*1½-inch piece fresh ginger,
coarsely chopped*

*⅔ cup rice wine or
apple cider vinegar*

¾ cup superfine sugar

⅔ cup water

*2 tablespoons crushed
red pepper flakes*

¼ teaspoon salt

1. Put the chiles, garlic, and ginger into a small food processor and pulse until finely chopped but not pureed, scraping down the sides as necessary. Alternatively, finely chop the chiles, garlic, and ginger with a sharp knife.

2. Add the vinegar, sugar, and water and blend together.

3. Transfer the ingredients to a heavy saucepan over high heat. Add the crushed red pepper flakes and salt, stirring to dissolve the sugar.

4. Bring to a boil, without stirring. Reduce the heat to medium–low and simmer, stirring frequently so the sauce doesn't stick to the bottom of the pan, for about 20 minutes, or until thickened.

5. Transfer the sauce to a bowl and let cool completely, stirring occasionally. The sauce can be used immediately, or stored in an airtight container in the refrigerator for up to two weeks.

Chipotle Pork Fajitas

These fabulous fajitas are great for sharing with a small gathering of friends. Once all the different elements are prepared and cooked, everyone can simply assemble their own fajitas and dig in.

SERVES 4
Prepares in 25 minutes
Cooks in 20–25 minutes

1 tablespoon ground chipotle chile
2 teaspoons packed light brown sugar
1 teaspoon salt
1 teaspoon ground cumin
1 teaspoon dried oregano
½ teaspoon garlic powder
1 pork tenderloin, cut into
   ½-inch strips
2 bacon strips, diced
1 tablespoon olive oil
1 onion, sliced
1 red bell pepper, chopped
1 yellow bell pepper, chopped
1 tablespoon garlic paste

To Serve
8–12 flour tortillas
salsa
guacamole or sliced avocado
sour cream
cilantro sprigs
lime wedges, for squeezing

1. Preheat the oven to 400°F.

2. Combine the ground chile, sugar, salt, cumin, oregano, and garlic powder in a small bowl.

3. Put the pork and bacon pieces into a large bowl with the spice mixture and toss until the meat is thoroughly coated in the spice mixture.

4. Heat the oil in a large skillet over medium–high heat. Add the pork and bacon (you may have to cook the meat in two batches to avoid overcrowding the pan) and cook, stirring, for 4–5 minutes, until the meat is browned. Transfer to a plate.

5. Add the onion, red bell pepper, yellow bell pepper, and garlic paste to the skillet and sauté for about 4 minutes, or until the vegetables begin to soften. Return the meat to the pan and heat until warmed and cooked through.

6. Meanwhile, wrap the tortillas in aluminum foil and put into the preheated oven to warm for 5 minutes.

7. Serve the pork mixture in a bowl alongside the warm tortillas, salsa, guacamole, sour cream, cilantro sprigs, and lime halves. Assemble the fajitas and eat while hot.

Colossal Lamb Kabob with Hot Chili Sauce

Grilled spicy lamb pieces are served on a warm flatbread and topped with hot chili sauce and yogurt to create this tantalizing Friday night dinner, ideal for one mighty appetite, but even better for two sharing.

MAKES 1
Prepares in 20 minutes
Cooks in 9–11 minutes

1 pound boneless leg of lamb, diced
2 tablespoons olive oil
1 teaspoon dried thyme
1 teaspoon paprika
1 teaspoon ground cumin
1 large flatbread
1 small red onion, sliced
1 tomato, chopped
small bunch fresh cilantro, chopped
½ lemon
salt and pepper
sriracha or other hot chili sauce
   and plain yogurt, to serve

1. Put the lamb with the olive oil, thyme, and spices into a medium bowl. Season to taste with salt and pepper and mix thoroughly to combine.

2. Preheat a large ridged grill pan or a barbecue grill.

3. Thread the lamb pieces onto two large skewers and cook in the preheated pan or on the grill rack for 4–5 minutes on each side, or until cooked through.

4. Heat a large, dry skillet and cook the flatbread for a few seconds on both sides until soft.

5. Remove the lamb from the skewers, place on the flatbread, and top with the onion, tomato and cilantro. Squeeze the lemon over the top and serve immediately drizzled with the sriracha and plain yogurt.

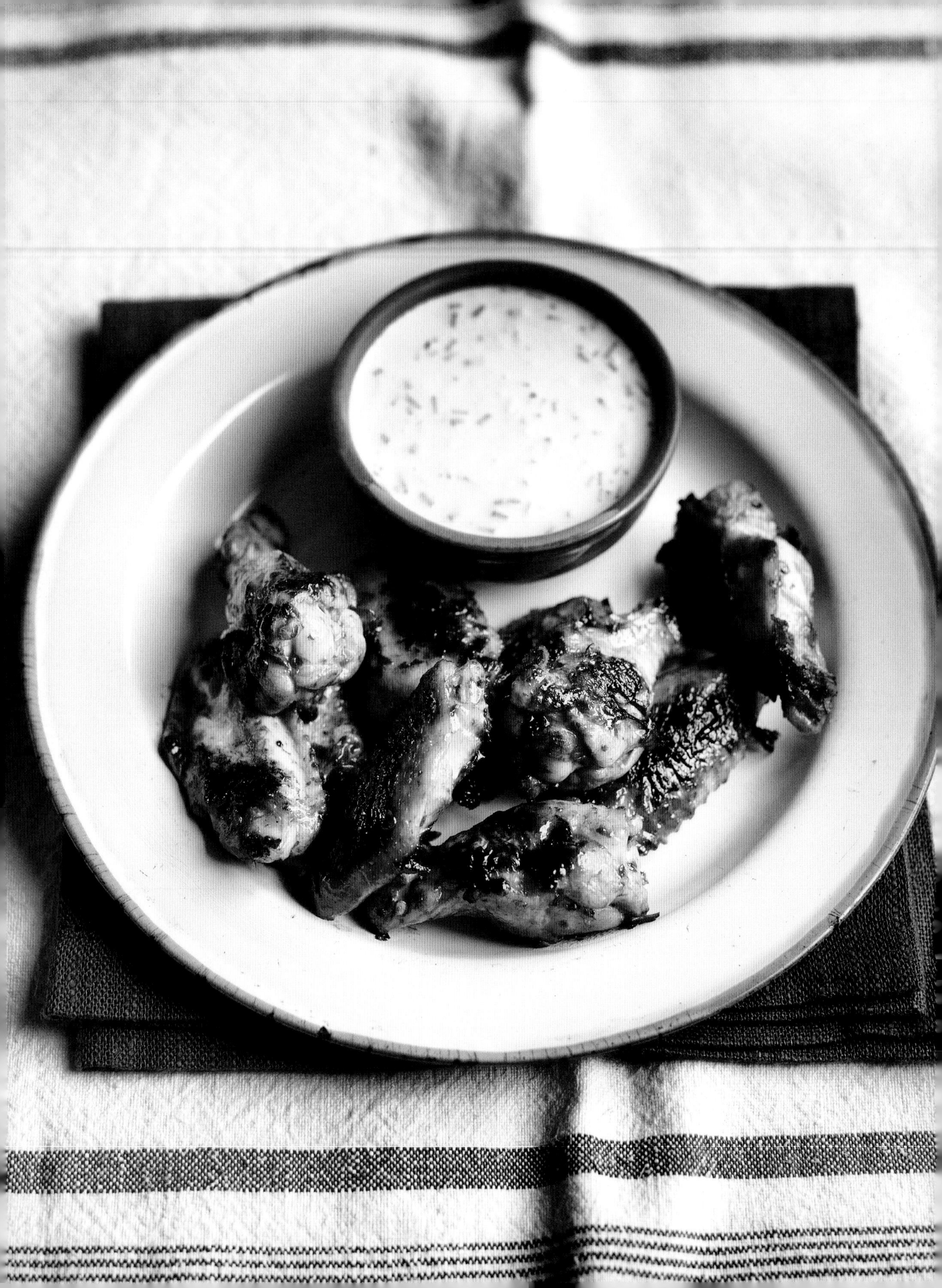

Blazing Hot Wings with Blue Cheese Dressing

If you are feeling weary after a hectic week at work, wake up your taste buds with these sizzling hot and spicy grilled chicken wings accompanied by a creamy blue cheese dressing. They are finger-licking good.

SERVES 4
Prepares in 30 minutes,
  plus marinating
Cooks in 30–35 minutes

¼ cup maple syrup
1 tablespoon hot pepper sauce
24 chicken wings, wing tips removed
  and each wing cut into two pieces
  at the "elbow" joint
sunflower oil, for brushing
salt and pepper

Blue Cheese Dressing
1 cup crumbled blue cheese
1 tablespoon English mustard
1¼ cups sour cream
2 tablespoons finely snipped fresh chives
salt and pepper

1. Combine the maple syrup and hot pepper sauce in a large bowl. Season to taste with salt and pepper.

2. Add the chicken wings to the bowl and rub the wings into the sauce mixture. Set aside at room temperature for 30 minutes. If making in advance, cover the bowl with plastic wrap and chill in the refrigerator until 30 minutes before cooking.

3. When ready to broil, preheat the broiler to high. Line the broiler tray with aluminum foil, shiny side up, and brush the rack with oil.

4. Arrange the chicken wing pieces on the broiler rack, fleshy side down. Position the rack 5 inches away from the heat and cook for 20 minutes, basting occasionally with any marinade left in the bowl.

5. Turn the chicken pieces over, baste, and continue to cook for 10–15 minutes, or until the skin is dark golden brown and the juices run clear when the thickest part of the meat is pierced with the tip of a sharp knife.

6. Meanwhile, to make the dressing, blend the cheese, mustard, and sour cream in a food processor. Stir in the chives and season to taste.

7. Serve the chicken wings hot, with the dressing on the side.

Savvy Pantry Ingredients

It's a good idea to keep a decent stock of pantry essentials, the type of ingredients that you use regularly in cooking. They will help to supply savvy solutions for putting together tasty meals after a hard week at work. Pantry spices, in particular, provide an easy and effective way to add maximum flavor to basic dishes with minimum effort, allowing you more time for unwinding and relaxing on a Friday night.

There is a vast variety of spices available, especially if you look in ethnic grocery stores, so choose them carefully and keep a small supply of spices that you use regularly in a kitchen cabinet, plus a modest selection of dried herbs, too. Popular dried spices ideal for the pantry include: allspice, caraway seeds, cardamom pods, cayenne, chile, cinnamon, cloves, coriander, cumin, curry paste or powder, fennel seeds, fenugreek seeds, garam masala, ginger, mustard seeds, nutmeg, paprika, smoked paprika, star anise, sumac, and turmeric. Dried herbs that are great as pantry standbys include: bay leaves, marjoram, mixed herbs, oregano, rosemary, sage, tarragon, and thyme.

To maximize the finest flavor from spices, buy good-quality whole spices and grind them yourself, using a clean electric coffee grinder (kept specifically for spices) or a spice grinder. Alternatively, you can use a mortar and pestle for grinding but you'll need some elbow grease to use them. It's best to buy whole spices in relatively small quantities, because they will gradually lose their flavor and become stale, and make sure you grind them fresh each time. If you do use store-bought ground spices, be sure to keep them in airtight containers or jars in a cool, dark, dry place, and replace them every six months or so, because they lose their fresh flavor quickly—the same applies to dried herbs, too.

Dry-frying whole spices in a heavy skillet for a few minutes, or until they release their delicious fragrances, before grinding them will also bring out their full aromatic flavor and vastly improve the taste of your dishes.

Indian and Chinese supermarkets are a great source for both fresh and dried spices and herbs, but nowadays many supermarkets or small stores stock a wide range, too, as do many delis and speciality online suppliers.

Store-bought dried spice blends or herb mixes are handy to have in case you don't have time to make them from scratch. These include: Cajun, Chinese five-spice powder, Creole, dukkah, fajita, herbes de Provence, Italian mixed herbs, Jamaican jerk, piri piri, ras-el-hanout, Thai seven-spice powder, and za'atar. Gourmet spice rubs and pastes are also great go-to flavor improvers if you are short of time.

It is useful to have some essential pantry staples in the cabinets at all times, so you can create dishes in no time. Try keeping a stocklist of these items so you know if you need to replace any when you go shopping.

These essentials include: canned tomatoes, corn kernels and beans; canned fish; condiments such as chili sauce, soy sauce, tomato paste, pesto, tomato puree or tomato sauce, smooth and grainy mustards, Worcestershire sauce, Thai fish sauce, and mayonnaise; a selection of dried beans, pasta, rice, grains, and lentils, including on-trend grains and seeds such as polenta, farro, spelt, and quinoa; sun-dried tomatoes; olives; jars of roasted red peppers and artichokes; good-quality bouillon powder or cubes; tahini; a small selection of different oils and vinegars; a selection of dried fruit, nuts, seeds, and pine nuts; sugars; and flours.

It's also a good idea to have some superior pantry ingredients on hand for more elaborate dishes or guests.

These might include: cold-pressed oils; good-quality balsamic vinegar; Kalamata olives; risotto rice; French lentils; sea salt flakes; harissa paste; nut oils for dressings; green peppercorns in liquid; Sichuan peppercorns; capers or caper berries; juniper berries; saffron; tamarind paste; anchovies; dried porcini; preserved truffles; pickled lemons; wasabi paste; vanilla beans; almond extract; orange flower water and rose water; maple syrup; preserved ginger; and good quality dark chocolate.

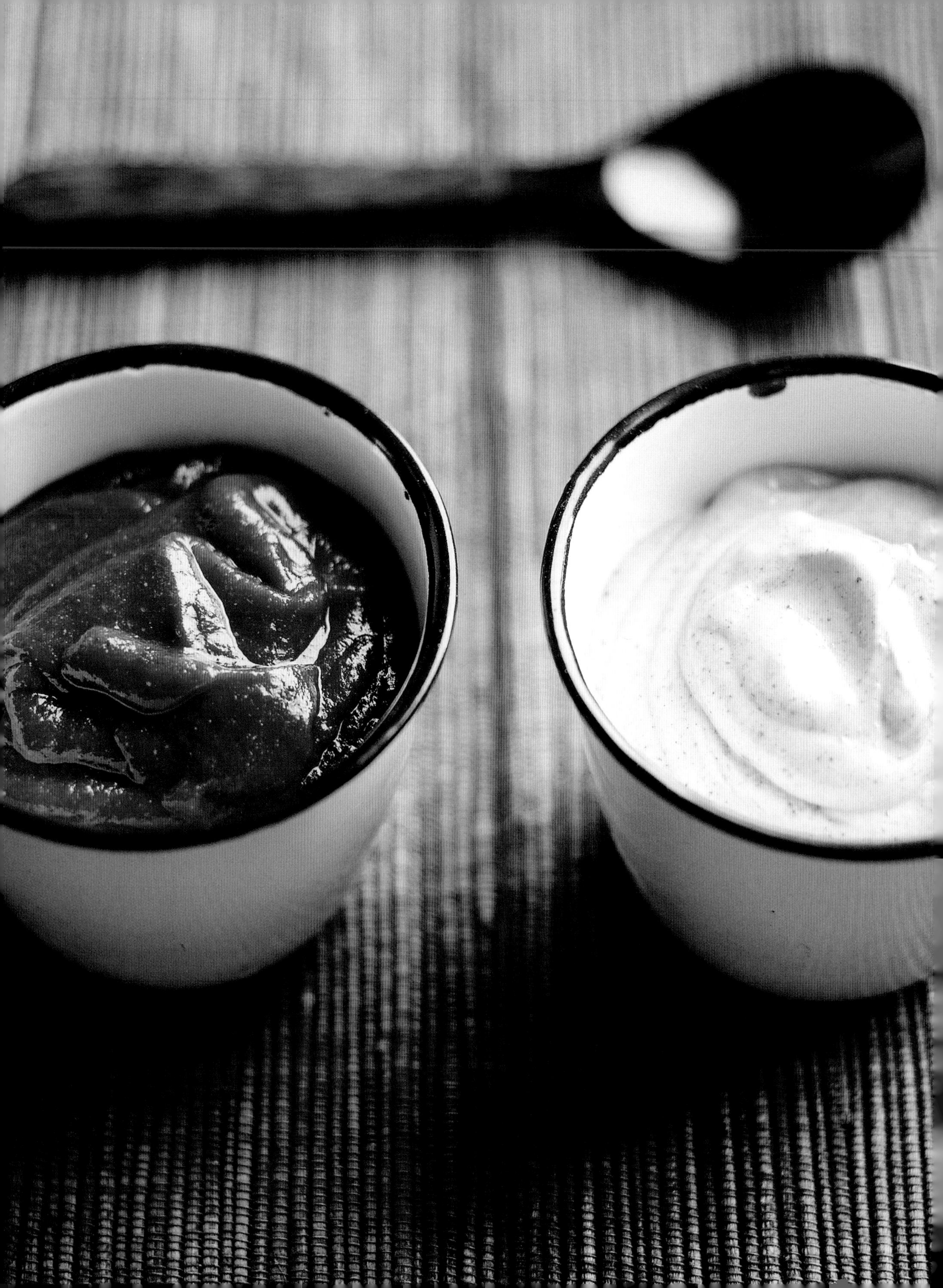

Chipotle Ketchup & Chipotle Mustard

Add some zing and spice to mealtimes with these two simple but sensational sides, perfect for serving with grilled or barbecued steaks, kabobs, burgers, or hotdogs, or chargrilled vegetables.

SERVES 8
Prepares in 15 minutes,
  plus cooling and chilling
Cooks in 5 minutes

Chipotle Ketchup

1 cup ketchup
½ teaspoon Worcestershire sauce
½ teaspoon packed light brown sugar
1 tablespoon fresh lemon juice, or to taste
1½ teaspoons ground chipotle chile
1 teaspoon ground cumin
½ teaspoon ground turmeric
¼ teaspoon ground ginger
salt

Chipotle Mustard

½ cup Dijon mustard
1 teaspoon ground chipotle chile

1. To make the ketchup, combine all of the ketchup ingredients, with salt to taste, in a small saucepan and put over medium heat. Bring to a simmer and cook, stirring frequently, for 5 minutes, or until the ketchup is slightly thickened.

2. Remove the saucepan from the heat and let cool. Transfer the ketchup to a sterilized jar, cover, and refrigerate until ready to use.

3. To make the chipotle mustard, put the ingredients into a small bowl and stir to thoroughly combine. Transfer to a sterilized jar, cover, and refrigerate until ready to use.

Rosemary, Sea Salt & Sesame Popcorn

SERVES 4

Prepares in 10–15 minutes

Cooks in 6–8 minutes

⅓ cup sesame seeds

2 tablespoons olive oil

2 rosemary stems

1 cup popping corn

1 teaspoon sea salt

2 tablespoons balsamic vinegar

1. Add the sesame seeds to a large skillet with 1 teaspoon of the oil, cover, and cook over medium heat for 2–3 minutes, shaking the pan from time to time, until the seeds are toasted golden brown and beginning to pop. Transfer from the pan to a bowl and wipe out the pan with a piece of paper towel.

2. Tear the rosemary into large pieces and add the remaining oil and the rosemary to the pan. Heat gently, shaking the pan to release the rosemary's oil. Add the corn, cover with the lid, and cook over medium heat for 3–4 minutes, shaking the pan, until all the popcorn has popped.

3. Remove from the heat and sprinkle with the toasted sesame seeds and season with the salt and vinegar, then transfer to a serving bowl, discarding the rosemary just before eating.

Root Vegetable Chips with Herb Yogurt Dip

SERVES 4

Prepares in 30–35 minutes, plus chilling and cooling

Cooks in 12–16 minutes

2¼ pounds mixed root vegetables, such as carrots, parsnips, sweet potatoes, or golden beets, very thinly sliced

¼ cup virgin olive oil

sea salt and pepper

Herb Yogurt Dip

1 cup Greek-style plain yogurt

2 garlic cloves, finely chopped

¼ cup finely chopped fresh herbs, such as flat-leaf parsley, chives, basil, or oregano

1. Preheat the oven to 400°F. To make the herb yogurt dip, spoon the yogurt into a small bowl, then stir in the garlic and herbs, and season with salt and pepper. Cover and chill in the refrigerator until ready to serve.

2. Put the vegetables into a large bowl. Slowly drizzle the oil over them, gently turning the vegetables as you work, until they are thoroughly coated.

3. Arrange the vegetables over three baking sheets in a single layer, then season with salt and pepper. Bake for 8–10 minutes, then check the chips—the slices in the corners of the sheets will cook more quickly, so transfer any that are crisp and golden to a wire rack. Cook the rest for an additional 2–3 minutes, then transfer any other cooked chips to the wire rack. Cook the remaining slices for an additional 2–3 minutes, if needed, then transfer any remaining chips to the wire rack and let cool.

4. Arrange the chips in a bowl and spoon the dip into a smaller bowl to serve.

Saturday Kick-Start
Breakfasts & Lunches

Whether you are an early riser who likes to power up for the day with an early morning workout or you prefer a more leisurely lie-in, Saturday morning should be about preparing for the rest of the weekend. This is the time to plan for the fun ahead and, if you haven't already done so, spend some time deciding what to cook and sourcing fresh ingredients, allowing yourself time to indulge your passion for creative cooking.

On a Saturday morning, give yourself plenty of time to plan and get ahead, so you are relaxed and ready to create a fabulous feast and enjoy an evening of entertaining friends or family. Prepare make-ahead dishes to serve later if you can, such as soup, pâté, ice cream, or sorbet, or why not bake some fresh bread for lunch or to accompany your evening meal?

All the recipes in this chapter will either help you to kick-start the day with a leisurely breakfast, or relish a relaxing lunch a little later, while enjoying the good company of those around you.

If your main focus is on fitness and you enjoy a Saturday morning workout, or perhaps you regularly go out for a run, cycle, or gym session, boost your energy levels before you go with one of our sensational Single Shot Juice Boosters or Beet Power Juice. You'll be off and running before you know it.

If you're more inclined to take things a little easier in the morning, then we include an appealing collection of breakfast recipes to get you going. Choose from classics, such as Creamy Oatmeal with Blackberries or Cranberry & Seed Muesli or, for something more substantial, there are global popular picks, such as The Best Bacon Hero Sandwich or Croque Monsieur, to start your day off perfectly.

If you prefer something sweet to accompany your morning mug of tea or coffee, then you could nibble your way through some warm Coffee & Pecan Mini Breakfast Muffins, or if you have guests staying over, the Coconut Flour Pancakes will go down well.

As lunch beckons a little later on and perhaps friends or family have joined you, tempt their taste buds with new favorites, such as Fish Stick Sandwiches, Turkey Wraps with Avocado Salsa, or simple but sophisticated Smoked Salmon Bagels. For vegetable lovers, Pea Soup with Blue Cheese & Croutons or Flatbread Pizzas with Zucchini Ribbons are bound to appeal. If you want to try a different type of grain, why not opt for the tempting Green Farro Salad with Feta?

Now is a good time to decide where you are eating your meal tonight and take time to set the table in readiness for your guests arriving later. If it looks set to be a balmy summer's day, then perhaps plan to eat alfresco later and make sure the backyard furniture is all set up and ready to use. On the other hand, if the weather has turned wet or wintry and there's a distinct dampness or chill in the air, stock up the wood store and get the wood burner or open fire ready to roar.

Greek-Style Yogurt with Orange Zest & Toasted Seeds

SERVES 2

Prepares in 10 minutes,
plus cooling

Cooks in 2–3 minutes

2 teaspoons flaxseed
2 teaspoons pumpkin seeds
2 teaspoons chia seeds
1 cup Greek-style plain yogurt
grated zest of 1 small orange,
plus 1 teaspoon juice

1. Put a small skillet over medium heat. When it is hot, add the flaxseed, pumpkin seeds, and chia seeds. Toast, stirring constantly with a wooden spoon, until they start to turn brown and release a nutty aroma. Transfer to a plate and let cool.

2. Spoon the yogurt into two glass jars or serving bowls, then sprinkle the seeds on top, followed by the orange zest. Sprinkle with the orange juice and serve immediately.

Creamy Oatmeal with Blackberries

SERVES 2
Prepares in 10–12 minutes
Cooks in 10 minutes

1¼ cups rolled oats
small pinch of sea salt
2½ cups cold water
3½ tablespoons heavy cream
1 tablespoon stevia or sugar to taste

To Serve
1 tablespoon pumpkin seeds
6 large blackberries, quartered
heavy cream, for pouring

1. Put the oats and salt into a medium saucepan and pour in the water. Bring to a boil, then reduce the heat to medium–low and simmer, stirring regularly, for 5–6 minutes, or until the oats are thick but have a dense pouring consistency.

2. Stir in the cream and stevia. Spoon the oatmeal into two bowls, top with the pumpkin seeds and blackberries, and serve immediately with a little extra cream for pouring over the top.

Coffee & Pecan Mini-Breakfast Muffins

MAKES 9

Prepares in 25 minutes, plus cooling

Cooks in 20 minutes

⅓ cup plus 1 tablespoon coconut flour

¼ teaspoon baking powder

½ teaspoon baking soda

1 tablespoon stevia

⅓ cup coarsely chopped pecans

⅔ cup sour cream

⅓ cup vegetable oil

2 extra-large eggs, beaten

⅓ cup prepared espresso or strong instant coffee

1 teaspoon rice malt syrup

salt

1. Preheat the oven to 325°F. Put nine mini muffin cups into a mini muffin pan.

2. Put the flour, baking powder, baking soda, stevia, 3 tablespoons of the pecans, and a small pinch of salt into a large bowl and mix well. Add the sour cream, oil, eggs, and ¼ cup of espresso, and stir until evenly mixed. Let stand for a moment, then spoon the batter into the mini muffin cups.

3. Bake in the preheated oven for 20 minutes, or until well risen and the tops spring back when pressed with a fingertip. Let cool slightly, then transfer to a wire rack.

4. To make the topping, put the syrup and remaining espresso into a bowl and mix. Spoon a small drizzle over each muffin. Sprinkle with the remaining pecans and serve warm, or store in an airtight container for up to two days.

Cranberry & Seed Muesli

SERVES 6

Prepares in 20 minutes,
plus soaking or chilling

No cooking

3 cups rolled oats

½ cup rye flakes

¾ cup coarsely chopped almonds

⅓ cup dried cranberries

2 tablespoons sunflower seeds

2 tablespoons pumpkin seeds

2 tablespoons flaxseed

2 crisp, sweet apples, such as Pippin,
cored and coarsely grated

1¾ cups fresh
apple juice, plus extra to serve

1. Put the oats, rye flakes, almonds,
cranberries, sunflower seeds,
pumpkin seeds, and flaxseed
into a large bowl and mix
well. Stir in the apples.

2. Add the apple juice, stir, cover,
and let soak for 1 hour, or chill
in the refrigerator overnight.

3. Spoon the mixture into six
serving bowls. Serve with a
small bowl of extra fresh apple
juice for pouring over the top.

Single Shot Juice Boosters

SERVES 1

Each prepares in 5 minutes

No cooking

Beet Booster

2 beets, halved

¼ cup chilled water (optional)

Kiwi Booster

2 kiwis

Blueberry Booster

1 cup blueberries

¼ cup chilled water

1. For the Beet Booster, feed the beets through a juicer. Pour into a glass, top up with the water, if using, and serve.

2. For the Kiwi Booster, feed the kiwis through a juicer. Pour into a glass and serve.

3. For the Blueberry Booster, put the blueberries and water in a blender, then process until smooth. Pour into a glass and serve.

Beet Power Juice

SERVES 1

Prepares in 10 minutes

No cooking

2 beets, halved

3 tablespoons flaxseed

4 plums, quartered and pitted

1 cup seedless red grapes

1 cup chilled water

ice, to serve (optional)

1. Feed the beets through a juicer. Put the flaxseed into a blender and process until finely ground.

2. Add the beet juice, plums, grapes, and water to the blender and process until smooth.

3. Pour the juice into a glass, add ice, if using, and serve immediately.

Coconut Flour Pancakes with Lemon Drizzle

These tasty pancakes made with coconut milk and coconut flour (and cooked in coconut oil!) will be a hit with any guests. The lemon drizzle, along with a dollop of crème fraîche, finishes them off perfectly.

SERVES 4
Prepares in 25–30 minutes
Cooks in 18 minutes

2 extra-large eggs
½ cup coconut milk
½ cup cold water
1 teaspoon vanilla extract
1 tablespoon stevia
½ cup coconut flour
1 teaspoon baking soda
1 tablespoon coconut oil
salt
¼ cup crème fraîche, to serve (optional)

Lemon Drizzle

finely grated zest and juice of 1 lemon
2 teaspoons rice malt syrup

1. Crack the eggs into a bowl, then add the coconut milk, water, vanilla, stevia, flour, and baking soda and season with a pinch of salt. Whisk to a smooth batter, then let rest for a moment.

2. Meanwhile, to make the lemon drizzle, put the lemon zest and juice and rice malt syrup into a small bowl and mix well.

3. Heat the coconut oil in a large skillet over medium heat. Pour in a tablespoon of the batter, let settle for a moment, then add more tablespoons, allowing a little space between each one.

4. Cook for 2 minutes, or until the bottom of each pancake is light brown and the sides are set. Carefully flip over the pancakes using a spatula and cook for an additional 2 minutes.

5. Transfer the pancakes to warm serving plates. Cook the remaining pancakes in the same way. Top each plate of pancakes with a tablespoon of crème fraîche, if using, and spoon the lemon drizzle over the top.

1   1   3

Huevos Rancheros

Create this popular and delicious Mexican breakfast dish at home with easy-to-find ingredients. It's an ideal hassle-free Saturday morning breakfast for two, good served on its own or with some warm fresh crusty bread.

SERVES 2
Prepares in 15 minutes
Cooks in 25 minutes

2 tablespoons olive oil
1 large onion, finely chopped
2 green or red bell peppers,
  coarsely chopped
1 garlic clove, finely chopped
½ teaspoon crushed red pepper flakes
4 plum tomatoes, peeled
  and coarsely chopped
2 eggs
salt and pepper

1. Heat the oil in a large, nonstick skillet. Add the onion and cook until golden. Add the bell peppers, garlic, and crushed red pepper flakes and cook until the bell peppers are soft.

2. Stir in the tomatoes and season to taste with salt and pepper. Put over low heat and simmer for 10 minutes.

3. Using the back of a spoon, make two depressions in the mixture in the skillet. Break the eggs into the depressions, season, cover, and cook for 3–4 minutes, or until the eggs are set. Serve immediately.

The Best Bacon Hero Sandwich

Crusty French bread, spread with mayo and stuffed full of crispy smoked bacon, then topped with fried eggs, melting Swiss cheese, and chipotle chili sauce. What better way can there be to kick-start the weekend?

MAKES 2
Prepares in 15–20 minutes
Cooks in 8–12 minutes

1 large French stick
¼ cup mayonnaise
1 pound smoked bacon
¼ cup vegetable oil
4 eggs
10 Swiss cheese slices
chipotle chili sauce, to taste

1. Preheat the broiler to high.

2. Cut the French stick in half lengthwise. Spread the insides of the bread with the mayonnaise and set the French stick aside.

3. Put the bacon onto a broiler pan and cook under the preheated broiler on both sides until crispy or cooked to your preference. Set aside in a warm place.

4. In a skillet, heat the oil over medium–low heat. Once hot, crack the eggs gently into the pan, one at a time. Cook the eggs until set, or to your preference.

5. Place the cheese slices on one half of the French stick and top with the bacon, fried eggs, and chipotle chili sauce.

6. Press the two halves of the French stick together gently. Cut in half and serve immediately.

Croque Monsieur Sandwich

SERVES 1
Prepares in 15 minutes
Cooks in 5–7 minutes

2 slices white bread, buttered
2 slices smoked ham
½ cup shredded Gruyère or Swiss cheese
pat of butter, melted
salt and pepper
lightly dressed mixed green salad, to serve

1. Preheat the broiler to high.

2. Lay one piece of bread, buttered side up, and place the ham on top. Cover with two-thirds of the cheese and season. Lay the other slice of bread on top, buttered side down. Brush the top side with the melted butter and place the sandwich, buttered side up, under the broiler.

3. Broil until browned, then take out from under the broiler. Turn the sandwich over and sprinkle the remaining cheese on top. Replace under the broiler and cook until the cheese is bubbling and browned. Remove and serve with a green salad.

Pea Soup with Blue Cheese & Croutons

SERVES 4
Prepares in 25 minutes
Cooks in 30–35 minutes

3 tablespoons unsalted butter
2 shallots, finely chopped
4 cups vegetable broth
2⅔ cups shelled peas
¼ cup crème fraîche or sour cream
salt and pepper
⅔ cup crumbled blue cheese, such as Roquefort, to serve

Croutons

2 slices whole-wheat bread, cut into cubes
2 tablespoons virgin olive oil

1. To make the croutons, preheat the oven to 300°F. Toss the bread cubes with the oil and sprinkle with ½ teaspoon of salt and ½ teaspoon of pepper. Arrange the cubes on a baking sheet in a single layer, then bake in the preheated oven for 25 minutes.

2. Meanwhile, to make the soup, melt the butter in a large saucepan over medium heat. Add the shallots and sauté, stirring, for 2–3 minutes, or until soft. Add the broth and peas, season with salt and pepper, then bring to a boil. Simmer for 15–20 minutes, or until the peas are tender.

3. Strain the peas through a strainer and reserve the cooking liquid. Transfer the peas to a food processor or blender and process into a puree, then return the mixture to the pan. Gradually stir in the cooking liquid until you have your desired consistency.

4. Reheat the soup. Stir in the crème fraîche and adjust the seasoning. Serve immediately, with the croutons and blue cheese sprinkled over the top.

Flatbread Pizzas with Zucchini Ribbons

These flatbread pizzas topped with zucchini ribbons, cherry tomatoes, and blobs of ricotta cheese will be a real hit with vegetarians. Great for a light lunch with a simple side of salad greens and a glass of something chilled.

SERVES 2
Prepares in 30 minutes
Cooks in 7–10 minutes

¼ cup crème fraîche
1 small–medium zucchini, shredded
 into ribbons using a vegetable peeler
4 cherry tomatoes, quartered
¼ cup ricotta cheese
1 garlic clove, crushed
2 tablespoons olive oil
salad greens, to serve (optional)

Pizza Crusts

¾ cup whole-wheat flour,
 plus extra for dusting
⅓ cup plus 1 tablespoon quinoa flour
¾ teaspoon baking soda
1 tablespoon olive oil
2 tablespoons warm water
salt

1. Preheat the oven to 400°F. To make the pizza crusts, put the flours and baking soda into a mixing bowl, season with salt, and stir. Add the oil, then gradually mix in enough of the warm water to make a soft but not sticky dough.

2. Lightly dust a work surface with flour. Knead the dough on the surface for 2 minutes, or until smooth and slightly elastic.

3. Put two large, flat baking sheets into the oven to get hot.

4. Divide the dough into two pieces. Roll out each piece to a circle about ¼ inch thick. Remove the hot baking sheets from the oven and, working quickly, lay the dough on top.

5. Spread the crème fraîche over the dough, then sprinkle with the zucchini and tomatoes. Blob the ricotta cheese in small dollops on top.

6. Bake the pizzas in the preheated oven for 7–10 minutes, or until the crusts are crispy and slightly puffed up, and the ricotta tinged golden.

7. Mix the garlic and oil together in a small bowl, and drizzle over the pizzas. Serve with salad greens, if using.

Fish Stick Sandwich with Russian Dressing

A simple but tasty lunch, this unusual version of a children's favorite is served with a spicy dressing and peppery arugula—it is sure to become a hit with a group of friends.

MAKES 2
Prepares in 15 minutes
Cooks in 20 minutes

oil, for deep-frying
20 fish sticks
4 large slices white bread
3½ cups arugula

Russian Dressing

2 tablespoons mayonnaise
1 tablespoon creamed horseradish
1 tablespoon ketchup
1 tablespoon sour cream
1 tablespoon sriracha hot chili sauce
1 teaspoon Worcestershire sauce
½ teaspoon smoked paprika

1. Put enough of the oil for deep-frying into a large, heavy saucepan or deep fryer. Heat the oil to 350–375°F, or until a cube of bread browns in 30 seconds.

2. Meanwhile, mix together all of the Russian dressing ingredients in a small bowl and set aside.

3. Deep-fry the fish sticks, in batches of ten, for 5 minutes or until golden, then remove with a slotted spoon. Drain on paper towels and let rest in a warm place while you cook the remaining fish sticks.

4. Spread some of the dressing on two of the bread slices. Divide the fish sticks between two slices of bread and drizzle with the rest of the dressing. Top with the arugula and the remaining bread slices and serve immediately.

Smoked Salmon Bagels

Once you have treated yourself and your pals to homemade bagels, you'll never buy store-bought ones again. Set some time aside in the morning to make these, then enjoy them warm for lunch with smoked salmon and cream cheese.

MAKES 12
Prepares in 35–40 minutes,
  plus standing, rising and
  cooling
Cooks in 20–25 minutes

1 tablespoon active dry yeast
2 tablespoons sugar
3½ tablespoons vegetable oil,
  plus extra for oiling
1 teaspoon salt
1 cup warm water
3⅓ cups all-purpose flour, plus
  extra for dusting
1 egg, beaten

1 egg, beaten with ¼ teaspoon salt,
  for glazing
poppy and sesame seeds, for sprinkling

Filling

smoked salmon
cream cheese
finely chopped fresh flat-leaf parsley
finely grated lemon zest

1. Combine the yeast and half of the sugar in a small bowl. Heat the remaining sugar, oil, salt, and water in a small saucepan for 1–2 minutes, or until warm and the sugar has dissolved. Pour into the yeast mixture, cover with a dish towel, and let stand for 5–7 minutes, or until the mixture begins to bubble. Put the flour into a food processor and, with the machine running, pour in the yeast mixture, then add the egg and process until a ball of dough forms.

2. Add a little more flour if the dough is sticky—it should be smooth and elastic. Lightly oil a large bowl and add the ball of dough, turning to coat on all sides to prevent a crust from forming. Cover with the dish towel and let rise in a warm place for 1½–2 hours, or until the dough has doubled in size. Turn out onto a lightly floured work surface. Knead lightly to deflate.

3. Divide the dough into 12 equal pieces. Roll each into a rope about 7 inches long and shape into a ring. Wet one end and press firmly to seal. Arrange on a floured baking sheet, cover with the dish towel, and let rise for 25 minutes, or until doubled in size. Meanwhile, preheat the oven to 400°F. Lightly oil two large baking sheets.

4. Bring a large saucepan of water to a boil. Working in batches, slide a few bagels into the water and cook for 1 minute. Remove with a slotted spoon and drain on paper towels.

5. Arrange the bagels on the baking sheets and carefully brush with the egg mixture. Sprinkle half with sesame seeds and the remainder with poppy seeds. Bake in the preheated oven for 12–15 minutes, or until golden and shiny. Remove and place on a wire rack to cool slightly. Serve warm with smoked salmon, cream cheese, parsley, and lemon zest.

Turkey Wraps with Avocado Salsa

These tasty turkey wraps are great for sharing, so once the turkey is marinated and the salsa is chopped, warm the tortillas and get broiling, so that everyone can get dig in and assemble their own wraps.

SERVES 4
Prepares in 30 minutes,
  plus marinating
Cooks in 12 minutres

4 thin turkey breast cutlets,
  about 12 ounces in total
olive oil, for brushing
4 romaine or lettuce leaves,
  thick stems removed, leaves sliced
  into ribbons
4 corn tortillas, warmed
3 tablespoons sour cream

Marinade
juice of 2 oranges
1 teaspoon cumin seeds, lightly crushed
½ teaspoon crushed red chile flakes
¼ cup olive oil
salt and pepper

Salsa
2 avocados, peeled, pitted,
  and diced
1 small red onion, diced
2 tomatoes, seeded and diced
2 tablespoons chopped fresh cilantro
juice of 1 lime

1. Slice the turkey cutlets into 1½ x 2½-inch strips. Put into a shallow dish.

2. To make the marinade, whisk together all the marinade ingredients. Pour the dressing over the turkey, cover, and marinate in the refrigerator for 4 hours, or overnight. Remove from the refrigerator at least 30 minutes before cooking to bring to room temperature.

3. To make the salsa, combine all the ingredients in a small bowl.

4. Preheat the broiler to high. Drain the turkey, discarding the marinade. Thread the strips concertina-style onto metal skewers (or use wooden skewers with aluminum foil wrapped around the ends so that they don't burn) and brush the turkey with oil.

5. Put the skewers onto a rack in the broiler pan and cook under the preheated broiler for about 5 minutes on each side, or until the turkey is cooked through and starting to brown at the edges. Check that the center of the meat is no longer pink and the juices run clear when the thickest part of the meat is cut through with a sharp knife. Remove the turkey from the skewers, set aside, and keep warm.

6. Divide the lettuce among the tortillas and arrange the turkey on top. Add a little sour cream and salsa. Roll the bottoms and sides of the tortillas over the filling and serve immediately.

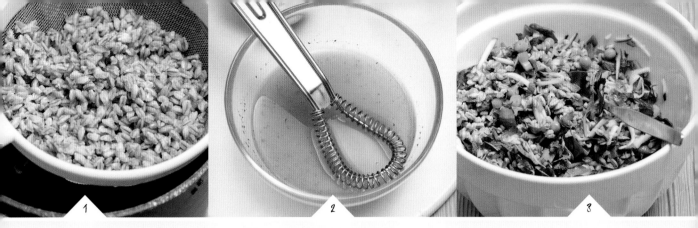

Green Farro Salad with Feta

Try a different grain and make this tempting salad of cooked farro, feta cheese, and vibrant green vegetables and herbs, all tossed together with a light lemony dressing.

SERVES 4
Prepares in 25 minutes,
  plus cooling and standing
Cooks in 15 minutes

1¼ cups quick-cooking farro, rinsed
½ teaspoon salt
⅓ cup fresh peas
5 scallions, some green included,
  thinly sliced
½ zucchini, coarsely grated
1¼ cups baby spinach, shredded
¼ cup chopped fresh mint leaves
¼ cup chopped fresh flat-leaf parsley
½ cup cubed feta cheese
sumac or paprika, for sprinkling

Dressing
2 tablespoons lemon juice
⅓ cup extra virgin olive oil,
  plus extra for drizzling
salt and pepper

1. Put the farro and salt into a saucepan with water to cover. Bring to a boil, then reduce the heat, cover, and simmer for 10 minutes, or until tender but still chewy. Drain, then spread out on a tray to cool slightly. Transfer to a serving bowl while still lukewarm.

2. To make the dressing, combine the lemon juice with salt and pepper to taste in a small bowl. Whisk in the oil. Pour the dressing over the farro and mix gently.

3. Stir in the peas, scallions, zucchini, spinach, mint, and parsley. Let stand at room temperature for 30 minutes.

4. Divide the mixture among four plates. Arrange the cheese on top, sprinkle with a little sumac, and drizzle with oil. Serve immediately.

Saturday Evening Specials

This inspirational chapter features a sensational selection of more elaborate dishes, ideal for entertaining and decadent dining. These recipes will help you showcase your finesse and flair in the kitchen and create first-rate dishes for everyone to enjoy. Make Saturday evening special—whether you are having a romantic meal or hosting an evening with friends.

As a competent and creative cook, you'll relish the challenge of trying something new, but especially when entertaining, don't try to cook out of your comfort zone or get too daunted by complicated techniques. Don't attempt to make too many dishes, otherwise a Saturday evening special may turn into a Saturday evening meltdown.

Choose and cook with seasonal ingredients if you can, because the taste will be so much better. Select dishes that reflect the time of year, too—choose warming, comforting dishes for chilly, wintry evenings and lighter, refreshing dishes for warm summer evenings. If you can prepare the appetizer or dessert ahead of time, you will have a little more time to spend with your companions.

When your guests arrive, offer a selection of tasty small bites, along with a glass of something chilled to get things going. If you really want to get the party started, serve some champagne, sparkling wine, or cocktails, such as Champagne Sidecar or Black Velvet, which are also great for sharing.

We include appealing appetizers and magnificent main dishes, followed by some truly decadent desserts. Tempting appetizers include first-class classics, such as Asparagus with Hollandaise Sauce, Marinated Baked Ricotta with Roasted Vegetables, and Roasted Duck Salad.

For the main event, prove your proficiency in the kitchen and transfer taste buds to all corners of the globe. For meat enthusiasts, select from elaborate eats, such as Asian Barbecued Cornish Game Hens or Pulled Pork with Mashed Sweet Potatoes. Fish and seafood aficionados are sure to enjoy Seared Scallops with Fresh Mint & Red Chile Dressing or Lobster Salad with Herb Mayonnaise. For those who prefer to eat less meat and fish, Kale, Lemon & Chive Linguine or Wild Mushroom Risotto are fitting for a special meal.

Serve some sophisticated sides alongside the main star, such as roasted potatoes, Swedish hasselback potatoes, scalloped potatoes (or Dauphinoise potatoes), hash browns, vegetable gratins, creamed vegetables, or creamy mashed vegetables. Alternatively, simple sides, such as steamed baby vegetables, tossed salads, stir-fried vegetables, or roasted roots, are ideal, especially if you are serving a rich and elaborate main dish.

Make sure you save space for an indulgent sweet treat and choose from one of our sumptuous sensations. Stunning desserts include Roasted Fig Tarts, Spiced Plum & Blackberry Brûlées, and Mocha Soufflés with Mascarpone. For committed chocoholics, individual Hot Chocolate Desserts & Candied Oranges will certainly hit the spot.

On a slightly lighter note, Champagne Sorbet will provide an elegant and refreshing dessert, ideal for cleansing the palate after an indulgent meal, but if cheese is more your thing, try Goat Cheese with Honey & Walnuts.

Finally, it's a good idea to have some after-dinner coffee options, so that you can provide a welcome hot drink to pep things up after the big meal. Some people may prefer a digestif or nightcap, such as a glass of cognac, whiskey, or port, or a liquor-base cocktail, such as a White Russian or Brandy Alexander, to help their meal go down and to finish the night off in style.

Creating the Perfect Dinner Party Menu

When planning a menu for a special meal, the key word is balance. The meal needs to feel as though it flows from beginning to end. You do not want your guests to feel too full at the end of the meal, but you do not want them to be hungry either, so it's a hard balancing act. If you do serve a rich dish, serve a lighter portion. If you feel the meal could be a little small, then perhaps think about serving bread or rolls.

Think about what food is going to be served before and after the main dish. With good food, less is often more. Leave your guests pleased and satisfied. If you are planning to have a creamy soup to start, you don't need to serve half a quart of the stuff to each person. Likewise, if you are serving your favorite rich chocolate cake for dessert, it can be a thin sliver instead of a great slab.

When deciding on what to cook, try not to have repetition of key ingredients, colors, or textures throughout the meal. If, for example, you decide to serve walnut bread with an appetizer of soup, followed by lamb with an almond stuffing and then a hazelnut chocolate pudding, you have an overwhelmingly nut-base menu. All the dishes are delicious, but there is no balance to the meal and the flavors are similar. You have also created another problem: If any of the diners happens to have a nut allergy, you will have to make an alternative option for every dish.

Another example of an unbalanced meal would be a cream of mushroom soup to start, followed by roasted chicken and creamed mashed potatoes and a dessert of crème caramel. You have created three delicious dishes in varying shades of pale brown, white, and cream, with little defining texture. Texture is vital to the creation of each dish as well as the overall balance of the meal.

Make sure that you don't serve only really soft food without any definition, because it can just seem too mushy.

When setting out to prepare a special meal, do make sure you give yourself enough time to enjoy creating and preparing it. The main focuses should be the cooking and having a good time, so try to get as much of the boring stuff done in advance so you can focus on being the chef and host for the evening. Do not try to leave work and then make an entire three-course dinner for guests who are arriving at 7:30 p.m. If you can shop the day before or during the day and maybe do some of the prep beforehand or make one of the dishes in advance, it will really make a great difference.

Dishes such as soups, casseroles, and curry pastes all lend themselves to being made in advance. Also some desserts can be made and then left to set in the refrigerator overnight. Then the dessert is guaranteed to be completely set and cold, which is one worry fewer for the evening, and you have managed to get at least one of the courses of the meal completely prepared in advance.

Before preparing the food, start by planning the order of preparation in an organized way that will work for you. In a kitchen, this is called time and

motion. You should have dishes baking in the oven or cooking slowly on the stove, or start any yeast-base bread and let cold desserts set, long before you do any last-minute jobs, such as chopping herbs.

When you are chopping, cleaning up, or setting the table, you are doing only one job at a time. However, if you have three or four other jobs going on at the same time, then doing that one job will not be a waste of time or slow you down. This will leave you more time to make your food look beautiful and really well thought out on the plate, so it's worth fully planning the evening out and organizing your time well in advance.

Another time-saver is to set the table in the morning or even the night before. You may find this a little excessive and superorganized, but in a restaurant, the tables for lunch are always set up straight after dinner the evening before. This is because it saves a huge amount of time and makes the meal that much easier to prepare and serve, because all the focus is on the food. This will make the evening as a whole much more enjoyable and relaxing, because at least you know that the table is ready. It also allows you to seat guests when they arrive so they are comfortable and enjoying a glass of wine while you finish off the last touches of preparation for the meal.

Getting Ready for a Dinner Party

It's Saturday evening and the guests are due any minute—you've got the wine perfectly chilled and the food is prepped and ready to go. It's time to put on some tunes and prepare for the fun and feasting ahead. Here is some advice on how to get the evening off to a great start and to keep the drinks, food, and conversation flowing effortlessly.

It is fine to have one dish that requires some last-minute cooking, such as scallops for a main dish. However, if every dish has a lot of last-minute cooking, you will spend the whole evening in the kitchen, missing out on all the conversations and apologizing to your guests for not being at the table with them.

Remember that herbs and salad greens should be prepped at the last minute, so that they do not wilt. Prep all similar ingredients at the same time. If garlic will be used in more than one dish, chop it as one batch, then use it as needed.

When choosing the cutlery and dinnerware that you will be using for each course, count them out into a pile. If you are cooking for four people, you should have enough matching plates, but if you are cooking for 12 or more, the quantities will be harder to keep tabs on.

It's fine to have to quickly wash the appetizer plates to be reused for dessert, because you should have time to do it, but if you don't have enough, try to borrow some dinnerware and cutlery from friends so you don't have to spend too long in the kitchen between dishes. Also, you don't want your guests to wait a long time for their main dish or dessert.

The type of dinnerware and the other table dressings are important for setting the right mood. Using candles or tealights can transform a simple dinner into something more stylish and sumptuous. Flowers on the table add color, although you should avoid strongly scented flowers, such as lilies, because they can overpower the aromas of the food.

Only use multicolored or patterned plates to serve something that has few colors. The rich red of a tomato soup could work in a blue patterned bowl. If your food has a lot of colors, shades, and shapes, it will sit much better on a plain white dish. The most elegant table settings are the most simple. Too many flavors on a plate do not make better food, and the same is true of presentation—too many contrasts of color and shape will over-complicate things and you will lose your focus.

Think about the colors and shapes and how they will best contrast and complement the plates and tableware. Some dishes, such as modern Asian food, may work on a square or rectangular plate, but not everything does. A dish from Spain, the Middle East, or Morocco will look good in a simple, glazed terra-cotta dish. More contemporary dishes will be better on large, flat white plates; other dishes will look better when served in slightly shallow, light-colored dishes.

1   2   3

Asparagus with Hollandaise Sauce

This classic dish makes a simple but impressive appetizer. Once you have mastered making your own smooth and creamy hollandaise sauce, it is also good for accompanying poached fish or broiled chicken, fish, or steaks.

SERVES 4
Prepares in 20–25 minutes, plus cooling
Cooks in 15 minutes

1½ pounds asparagus, trimmed

Hollandaise Sauce

¼ cup white wine vinegar
1½ teaspoons finely chopped shallots
5 black peppercorns
1 bay leaf
3 extra-large egg yolks
1¼ sticks unsalted butter, finely diced
2 teaspoons lemon juice
salt
pinch of cayenne pepper

1. Divide the asparagus into four bundles and tie each with kitchen twine, crisscrossing the twine from just below the tips to the bottom. Stand the bundles upright in a deep saucepan. Add boiling water to come three-quarters of the way up the stems, then cover with a loose tent of aluminum foil, shiny side down, inside the pan. Heat the water until bubbles appear around the side of the pan, then simmer for 10 minutes, or until the stems are just tender when pierced with the tip of a sharp knife. Drain well and remove the twine.

2. Meanwhile, to make the hollandaise sauce, boil the vinegar, shallots, peppercorns, and bay leaf in a saucepan over high heat until reduced to 1 tablespoon. Cool slightly, then strain into a heatproof bowl that will fit over a saucepan of simmering water.

3. Beat the egg yolks into the bowl. Set the bowl over the pan of simmering water and whisk the egg yolks constantly until they are thick enough to leave a trail on the surface.

4. Be careful to avoid letting the water boil. Gradually beat in the butter, piece by piece, whisking constantly until the sauce is like soft mayonnaise. Stir in the lemon juice, then add salt to taste and the cayenne pepper. Serve the sauce immediately with the asparagus.

Baked Seafood with Fresh Cilantro Chutney

These packages make a great start to a meal, because everyone receives their own package and then gets to experience opening it. There is great contrast between the bright green sauce and the pink shrimp.

SERVES 4
Prepares in 30 minutes,
  plus standing and cleaning
Cooks in 12 minutes

12 large shrimp, peeled and deveined
2¼ pounds live mussels, scrubbed
  and debearded
8 scallops
1 pound firm white fish, such as sea
  bream, halibut, or red snapper,
  skinned and cubed
vegetable oil, for greasing
salt and pepper

Cilantro Chutney
1⅔ cups dry unsweetened coconut
2 teaspoons coriander seeds
1 garlic clove, finely chopped

1-inch piece of fresh ginger, chopped
½ teaspoon salt
1 green chile, seeded and
  finely chopped
½ bunch of fresh cilantro
½ cup coconut milk
juice of 1 lime

1. For the chutney, cover the dry coconut with boiling water and let stand for 40 minutes. Roast the coriander seeds in a dry skillet over medium heat for 2 minutes, until fragrant. Be careful to avoid scorching them.

2. Crush the roasted coriander seeds. Put into a food processor with the garlic, ginger, and salt and work into a coarse paste. Add the chile and blend until smooth. Strain the coconut, reserving the soaking liquid. Add the coconut to the blender with two-thirds of the fresh cilantro.

3. Continue to blend this mixture until smooth and bright green. Add some of the coconut soaking liquid to help combine the mixture. Remove the mixture and put into a bowl. Stir in the coconut milk and lime juice. Taste and adjust the seasoning. This chutney is best used fresh, but it will keep, covered, in the refrigerator for a couple of days.

4. You could use any combination of seafood, such as shrimp, crayfish, lobster, crab, squid, mussels, and fish. Make sure the fish is cleaned, boned, and scaled and the shellfish is cleaned. Wash the shellfish until the water runs completely clear. Remove any shellfish that does not close when you tap them and remove any that smell.

5. To make the packages, fold a large rectangle of parchment paper in half, so the two shorter ends meet. Fold in half again, so that the two shorter ends meet. Hold by the two shorter ends and fold each end over slightly, by about 1 inch. You should have an envelope that is open at one end with two folded edges at the sides. Repeat with three other parchment paper rectangles. Rub a little oil on the inside of the envelopes. Season the seafood with a little salt and pepper.

6. Preheat the oven to 400°F and preheat two baking sheets. Mix the chutney with the seafood and then divide the mixture among the envelopes. Fold the open end of each envelope tightly to seal. These envelopes could be made, filled, and kept in the refrigerator for a couple of hours before you need them. Place the filled envelopes flat on the preheated baking sheets and bake in the preheated oven for 10 minutes.

7. When ready to serve, transfer the packages to plates and let your guests open them so that they get all the aromas. Warn them to be careful with the steam, because it may come out in a jet. Any shellfish that still has not opened should be discarded. Garnish the packages with the remaining fresh cilantro.

Marinated Baked Ricotta with Roasted Vegetables

Marinated fresh ricotta cheese and roasted mixed vegetables combine beautifully with a zingy lemon-herb dressing to create this mouthwatering meat-free salad, excellent served as a sensational appetizer before a meaty main dish.

SERVES 6
Prepares in 50 minutes,
 plus cooling
Cooks in 35 minutes

2 whole (7-ounce) ricotta cheeses
2 sweet potatoes, cut into
 1¼-inch cubes
1 butternut squash, cut into
 1¼-inch cubes
2 fennel bulbs
⅔ cup pine nuts
2 handfuls mixed bitter
 and peppery salad greens
olive oil
salt and pepper

Marinade
½ red chile
3 tablespoons olive oil
juice of 1 lemon

Dressing
½ garlic clove, finely chopped
pinch of salt
small bunch of fresh basil,
 coarsely chopped, plus extra leaves
juice and zest of 1 lemon
¼ cup extra virgin olive oil

1. Preheat the oven to 400°F. For the marinade, seed and finely chop the chile, then mix with the olive oil and lemon juice.

2. Add the whole ricotta cheeses to the marinade. Turn the cheeses regularly in the marinade. Brush the cubes of sweet potatoes and butternut squash with a little oil and season with salt and pepper. Place in a roasting pan and roast in the oven for about 20 minutes, until caramelized and golden.

3. Halve the fennel bulbs, removing the tough outside layer, then carefully chop each half into thin wedges.

4. Dry-roast the pine nuts on a separate baking sheet in the preheated oven and roast until golden brown.

5. For the dressing, crush the garlic with the salt to a fine puree. Put the garlic and most of the chopped basil into a food processor and pulse to a paste. Add the lemon juice and zest and work until smooth, and then stir in the olive oil (or you can use some of the oil from the marinade). Check the seasoning and add more salt and pepper to taste.

6. Heat an ovenproof skillet over medium–high heat. Add the whole ricotta cheeses and brown on one side for 2–3 minutes. Gently turn over—if it's too fragile to turn, just brown on one side. Sprinkle the fennel around the pan, season well with salt and pepper, and transfer to the oven for 5 minutes.

7. When the sweet potatoes and butternut squash are cooked (they should be soft when tested with the tip of a sharp knife) let cool slightly, then put into a bowl and dress with two-thirds of the basil dressing. Add the salad greens, tearing any that are too big. Tear and add the extra basil leaves. If you add the herbs to the salad just before serving, you will get the aromas and perfumes of the herbs. Add the fennel and then gently break in the ricotta cheese. Mix together lightly to avoid it turning mushy.

8. Place a 3½-inch round cookie cutter or ring on each plate and gently fill with the roasted vegetables and mixed salad. Pour the remaining dressing over the salad and garnish with the remaining chopped basil and roasted pine nuts. Remove the cutters and serve immediately.

Roasted Duck Salad with Orange & Warm Hazelnut Vinaigrette

Succulent roasted duck breasts
and juicy fresh orange sections
create the perfect pairing, while
roasted hazelnuts, watercress,
and mint leaves add extra
crunch and flavor to this
tantalizing warm salad starter.

SERVES 4–6
Prepares in 35–40 minutes
Cooks in 30 minutres

2–3 duck breasts
1 cup hazelnuts
2 bunches of watercress
4 oranges, peeled, sections separated,
  and pith removed
30 fresh mint leaves, plus extra to garnish
4 shallots, halved and finely sliced
salt and pepper

Vinaigrette
¼ cup orange juice
1 tablespoon fresh thyme leaves
¼ cup extra virgin olive oil
2 tablespoons red wine vinegar
2 tablespoons hazelnut oil or walnut oil
salt and pepper

1. Preheat the oven to 400°F. Trim the excess fat off of the duck breasts and season to taste with salt and pepper.

2. Put the duck breasts, skin side down, into a skillet over low heat. Cook for about 15 minutes, or until the skin is crisp and the fat is gone. Strain off any excess fat while you are cooking.

3. Roast the hazelnuts on a baking sheet in the preheated oven for about 5 minutes, or until the nuts have turned a golden brown.

4. Put the roasted nuts into a clean dish towel and rub vigorously to remove the skins. Put into a food processor and pulse until the nuts are coarsely chopped.

5. Season the duck breasts again with salt and pepper to taste and put them, flesh side down, into a roasting pan. Roast the duck in the preheated oven for 8 minutes, or until completely cooked through. Check that the center of the meat is no longer pink and that the juices run clear when the thickest part of the meat is pierced with the tip of a sharp knife—they should be cooked to medium.

6. Remove the duck breasts from the oven and let rest.

7. Put the vinaigrette ingredients into a small saucepan and put over low heat until warm. Do not let boil. When ready to serve, put the watercress into the bowl with the orange sections. Tear and add the mint and add the sliced shallots.

8. Thinly slice the warm duck breasts. Add to the bowl. Add any juices from the duck breasts to the vinaigrette.

9. Add half of the chopped hazelnuts to the vinaigrette.

10. Serve the salad on individual plates, building up layers of oranges, salad greens, slices of duck, and most of the remaining hazelnuts. Spoon the warm dressing over the top and then garnish each dish with any remaining chopped nuts and some torn mint.

Top Ten Styling Tips

A meal that is well presented with a visual flair can make all the difference to your enjoyment of the food. Learn how to serve your food with style, with the help of these hints and tips, which are simple but can add real appeal to your dishes.

1. Think of the plate or dish that you are serving on as though it were a picture frame—and remember that it has to suit the picture you have painted.

2. Plate regional food that is from particular countries or particular areas on plates, dishes, and platters that come from those regions, or have the same look.

3. Too many colors and patterns on dinnerware or table accessories will take the focus off the food. It's better to keep it simple instead of overcomplicating the color theme.

4. Keep your food styling simple and elegant so that you let nature's produce, and your hard work, speak for themselves.

5. Candles and tealights can soften the mood and make a table look more elegant. If you have to use electric lights, see if they can be dimmed or use small lamps that are less harsh. Colored glass Moroccan-style tealight holders or Asian paper lanterns can also create a great atmosphere for eating.

6. For the most effective results, carry a simple color theme through the table accessories, such as the napkins and flowers. For example, you could have a white tablecloth, blue and white napkins, and blue and white flowers on the table to add a really simple splash of color to a setting.

7. Make sure you clean away any fingerprints and splashes of gravy or sauce from the edges of the plates for a really professional finish. In restaurants, they use a clean cloth dipped in a mixture of water and a little vinegar. The acid cleans away grease instead of just spreading any oil around the edges of the plates.

8. When plating food, place it in the center of the plate and build up the layers of texture to create some height centered on the plate. You don't want your food to look like the leaning tower of Pisa, so aim for layers that are rising elegantly to a centered point.

9. When plating dishes for a lot of people at a buffet or a barbecue, use flat dishes and plates instead of bowls. It will be more visually appealing to look up at something, than to look down at something in the bottom of a bowl.

10. When arranging a number of larger dishes on a buffet table, vary the eye line to draw attention to the different types of food. Place some upside-down bowls or books under the tablecloth to create raised plinths for highlighting certain dishes that you think are extra special.

Top Ten Garnishing Tips

Garnishing can add real color and style to your finished dishes. Just a simple dash of chopped herbs can dress up a dish that was in danger of looking drab and brown. Style up your food with these top garnishing tips.

1. Let simple contrasting colors draw the eye to the food—for example, simple combinations, such as red with white or orange with white, can be effective and eye-catching.

2. Use texture to your advantage to create irregular textural differences that are visually exciting. The reason canned fruit salad looks so unappealing is because the contents are all uniform in size. When making a salad, cut each fruit or vegetable in a different way so that the eye will be drawn to the variations in shape and size.

3. Present things in uneven numbers, for example, three or five scallops. When things are presented in uneven numbers, your eye is interested and your brain is stimulated by the imperfection.

4. Let the ingredients in the dish form part of the garnish, for example chopped roasted nuts or pomegranate seeds, or torn mint or cilantro leaves. This creates a consistency of flavors, as well as adding visual appeal.

5. Use brightly colored ingredients, such as beet, pumpkin, and sweet potato, and colored spices, such as saffron and turmeric, to add a naturally colorful garnish to dishes.

6. Use fresh herbs to make some flavored, colored oils and dressings, such as basil or cilantro oil. They can be drizzled attractively over dishes to add color and style.

7. For straightforward and professional-looking dressing of a plate, buy some small, clear squeeze bottles. Any sauces or dressings can be poured into the bottle and applied neatly to the plate with a flick of the wrist.

8. Let the naturally beautiful form of an ingredient be appreciated for its own merits when serving foods, such as cooked mushrooms, slices of fennel, halved figs, and asparagus spears. These are shaped in a visually appealing way, so they look great just as they are.

9. Keep the number of components in a dish to a minimum, so that each piece has a relevance and adds an appropriate balance to the overall dish. Overcrowded dishes can look automatically less stylish.

10. Certain ingredients, such as honey, caramel, or oil, can make the elements of the most plain dish look bright and vibrant and sumptuous. Think of how beautiful plain yogurt simply drizzled with honey can be. Dress the dish with the sauce or dressing just before you serve it for the best effect.

Rib-Eye Steak, Chimichurri Sauce & Mashed Sweet Potatoes

Piquant chimichurri sauce complements the grilled rib-eye steaks perfectly in this tempting main dish for two. Accompanied by creamy mashed sweet potatoes, this is a great date-night meal.

SERVES 2
Prepares in 30 minutes
Cooks in 25–30 minutes,
  plus resting

1 tablespoon olive oil
2 rib-eye steaks, about 4½ ounces each
½ teaspoon ground cumin
salt and pepper

Chimichurri Sauce
¼ cup coarsely chopped fresh
  flat-leaf parsley
2 tablespoons fresh oregano
3 small garlic cloves, coarsely chopped
½ shallot, coarsely chopped
¼ red chile, seeded
  and coarsely chopped

3 tablespoons extra virgin olive oil
1 teaspoon red wine vinegar
juice of ¼ lemon

Mashed Sweet Potatoes
2 small sweet potatoes,
  cut into ¾-inch chunks
1½ tablespoons butter

1. To make the mashed sweet potatoes, cook the sweet potatoes in a large saucepan of lightly salted boiling water for 12–15 minutes, or until soft. Drain, then take off the heat to steam dry in the pan for at least 5 minutes. Using a potato masher, mash the potatoes to a smooth consistency.

2. Meanwhile, to make the chimichurri sauce, put all the ingredients in a food processor, season with salt and pepper, and process until you have a paste of a similar consistency to pesto. Add a little extra olive oil if the mixture appears too thick. Spoon into a serving bowl, cover, and set aside.

3. Return the mashed sweet potatoes to the heat and warm through before stirring in the butter. Season with salt and pepper and keep warm.

4. Massage the oil into both sides of each steak, then sprinkle with salt and the cumin. Heat a ridged grill pan over high heat until smoking hot. Cook each steak for 2–3 minutes on each side, or for longer if you prefer it well done. Let the steaks rest for 2 minutes.

5. Serve a steak on each of two plates with the chimichurri sauce spooned over and the mashed sweet potatoes on the side.

Slow-Cooked Lamb Shanks with Gremolata

These really flavorful slow-cooked lamb shanks are given a tantalizing twist with a sprinkling of roasted almond gremolata just before serving.

SERVES 4
Prepares in 25–30 minutes
Cooks in 2 hours 55 minutes

4 trimmed lamb shanks
2 tablespoons olive oil
4 garlic cloves, halved
1 dried chile, crushed
3 rosemary sprigs
6 ripe plum tomatoes
2 large onions, finely chopped
4 strips orange zest
2 bay leaves
1 teaspoon packed brown sugar
½ cup red wine
2 cups water
salt and pepper

Gremolata

1 cup blanched skinless almonds
2 garlic cloves, minced
zest of 2 lemons
small bunch of fresh flat-leaf parsley, chopped

1. Preheat the oven to 350°F. Season the lamb shanks well with salt and pepper. Heat 1 tablespoon of the oil in a large Dutch oven or heavy flameproof casserole dish. Add the meat to the pot and brown on all sides for 3 minutes, then remove from the heat. Chop the garlic, chile, and rosemary together.

2. Cut the tomatoes in half and, with the skin side in your hand, grate the flesh on a cheese grater to form a coarse tomato pulp. The skin will be left in your hand.

3. Remove the meat from the pot and return the pot to the heat with 1 tablespoon of the oil. Add the garlic, chile, and rosemary and sauté briskly for 2 minutes, or until fragrant and aromatic. Add the onions to the pot and sauté for about 5 minutes, or until soft. Season to taste with with salt and pepper.

4. Return the meat to the pot with the orange zest, bay leaves, sugar, tomato pulp, wine, and water. Stir until everything is thoroughly combined.

5. Cover and bring the mixture to a simmer over medium–high heat on the stove. Transfer the pot to the preheated oven and cook for an additional 2½ hours, basting regularly. Check the seasoning again and add more salt and pepper, if desired.

6. Meanwhile, to make the gremolata, roast the almonds in the preheated oven for 3 minutes, or until golden brown.

7. Make sure the garlic is really finely chopped, because it will be eaten raw. Put the minced garlic into a small bowl. Add the cooled almonds and the lemon zest to the bowl and mix to thoroughly combine.

8. When ready to serve, mix the parsley into the gremolata. Sprinkle the gremolata over the cooked lamb shanks and serve immediately.

Asian Barbecued Cornish Game Hens

Ideal for alfresco summertime eating, prepare these marinated Cornish game hens in advance, then simply barbecue them when you are ready to eat. Served with a tangy salad, this fantastic flavorful dish will thrill your guests.

SERVES 4

Prepares in 35–40 minutes, plus marinating

Cooks in 40–50 minutes, plus resting

2 Cornish game hens, about 1 pound each, butterflied

1 orange, thinly sliced

¼ cup extra virgin olive oil, plus extra for oiling

1½ tablespoons fresh orange juice

1 teaspoon sesame oil

4 bunches of fresh watercress leaves, trimmed, rinsed, and thoroughly dried, or 4 cups of other peppery salad greens

1 red bell pepper, thinly shredded with a vegetable peeler

2 tablespoons sesame seeds, toasted

salt and pepper

chopped fresh cilantro, to garnish

Marinade

⅓ cup sunflower oil

¼ cup soy sauce

2 tablespoons sesame oil

2 garlic cloves, very finely chopped

½-inch piece fresh ginger, grated

pinch of crushed red pepper flakes, to taste

1. To make the marinade, mix all the ingredients together in a nonmetallic bowl large enough to hold both hens, then set aside.

2. Ease the skin from the breast flesh on both birds. Gently slide the orange slices under the skin, then ease the skin back over the slices. Put the hens into the marinade and rub the mixture all over. Cover with plastic wrap and let marinate in the refrigerator for 4–24 hours, turning occasionally.

3. Remove the hens from the refrigerator 20 minutes in advance of cooking.

4. Preheat the barbecue. Brush the barbecue rack with olive oil and position it about 4 inches above the heat. Spear each bird with two long metal skewers, from left to right at the top and bottom, to keep them flat.

5. Put the birds on the grill rack, breast side down, and grill for 20–25 minutes on each side, basting occasionally with the remaining marinade. Grill until the birds are cooked through and the juices run clear when the thickest part of the thighs are pierced with the tip of a sharp knife or a skewer and there is no pink meat.

6. Let rest for 10 minutes, then cut each bird in half and remove the orange slices.

7. Alternatively, preheat the oven to 350°F. Heat a large ridged cast-iron grill pan over high heat until a splash of water "dances" on the surface. Brush with olive oil, then add the unskewered birds and grill for 10 minutes, or until browned.

8. Turn the birds over and put the pan into the preheated oven for an additional 30 minutes, basting occasionally with the remaining marinade, until the juices run clear when the thickest parts of the thighs are pierced with the tip of a sharp knife and there is no pink meat.

9. Meanwhile, mix the olive oil, orange juice, and sesame oil with salt and pepper to taste in a nonmetallic bowl. Add the watercress, bell pepper, and sesame seeds and toss together.

10. Arrange a portion of salad on each plate and serve with half a hen on top. Sprinkle with cilantro and serve hot or at room temperature.

Hearty Beef Stew with Herb-Cheese Dumplings & Kale

A warming, comforting dish using seasonal ingredients that is perfect for a cold winter evening. Get the fire roaring, break out a bottle of full-bodied red wine, and this stew is sure to hit the spot with any hungry guests.

SERVES 4
Prepares in 40 minutes
Cooks in 2 hours 55 minutes–
  3 hours 25 minutes

¼ cup olive oil
½ onion, finely chopped
1 leek, thinly sliced
1 celery stalk, coarsely chopped
4 garlic cloves, finely chopped
1 teaspoon tomato paste
2 pounds beef shank, cut into
  bite-size chunks
⅓ cup quinoa flour
½ cup brandy
3⅓ cups beef broth
1 tablespoon fresh thyme leaves
2 tablespoons finely chopped fresh
  flat-leaf parsley
2 teaspoons smoked paprika
6 cloves

2 bay leaves
salt and pepper
3 cups coarsely chopped kale, to serve
juice of ¼ lemon, to serve

Dumplings

1 cup quinoa flour
1 tablespoon beef suet or lard
½ cup shredded cheddar cheese
1 teaspoon baking powder
1 tablespoon fresh thyme leaves
2 tablespoons finely chopped fresh
  flat-leaf parsley
¼ cup water

1. Heat 2 tablespoons of the oil in a large lidded Dutch oven or casserole dish over medium heat. Add the onion, leek, and celery and sauté for 5 minutes, or until softened.

2. Add the garlic and tomato paste, stir well, then turn the heat down to medium–low and let simmer while you cook the meat.

3. Heat the remaining 2 tablespoons of the oil in a large, heavy skillet over high heat until smoking hot. Season the beef with salt and pepper, then add it to the pan, in batches, and cook for a few minutes, turning, until browned on all sides.

4. Using a slotted spoon, transfer the first batch to a plate while you brown the rest of the meat. Toss the browned meat into the Dutch oven, then stir in the quinoa flour.

5. Turn the heat down to medium–high. Deglaze the beef skillet with the brandy, being careful because it can ignite. Scrape all the meaty goodness off the bottom of the pan into the bubbling brandy with a wooden spoon, then add to the Dutch oven. Pour in the broth, then add the thyme, parsley, paprika, cloves, and bay leaves and season with salt and pepper.

6. Bring to a boil, then turn the heat down to low and cover. Simmer for 2–2½ hours, or until the sauce is thick and the meat is soft enough to pull apart with a spoon.

7. To make the dumplings, put the quinoa flour, suet, cheese, baking powder, thyme, and parsley into a large bowl and mix well. Add the water, a little at a time and mixing, until you have a firm dough. Shape the mixture into 12 small balls.

8. After 2–2½ hours cooking, remove the lid from the stew and arrange the dumplings on top. Put the lid back on and cook for 20 minutes, or until the dumplings are cooked through.

9. Cook the kale in a large saucepan of lightly salted boiling water for 2 minutes. Drain, then squeeze the lemon juice over the leaves and toss lightly. Serve immediately with the stew.

Barbecue Pulled Pork with Mashed Sweet Potatoes

Slow-cooked barbecued pork produces really tender, juicy shreds of tasty meat, which is then tossed in homemade chili sauce and served with mashed sweet potatoes. Perfect for outdoor summer eating with family or a group of friends.

SERVES 6–8
Prepares in 35–40 minutes
Cooks in 12 hours 20 minutes,
　plus resting

6½-pound pork shoulder,
　skin removed and bone in

Rub

1 tablespoon paprika
2 tablespoons packed light brown sugar
1 teaspoon dried thyme
1 teaspoon dried oregano
2 teaspoons pepper
1 teaspoon garlic salt
1 teaspoon celery salt
1 teaspoon salt
1 teaspoon onion powder

Chili sauce

2 tablespoons yellow mustard
2 tablespoons apple cider vinegar
2 tablespoons molasses
2 tablespoons ketchup
1 tablespoon sriracha chili sauce

Mashed Sweet Potatoes

5–6 sweet potatoes (about 2¼ pounds),
　diced
1¾ sticks salted butter, diced
1 teaspoon pepper

1. Preheat the barbecue grill to low heat.

2. Combine all of the rub ingredients together in a small bowl.

3. Put the pork onto a cutting board and massage the rub all over the surface of the pork.

4. Place the pork on the grill rack, making sure the pork is fat side up. Close the lid and cook for 12 hours, or until a thick, dark golden crust has formed and a meat thermometer reads 165–170°F. Or, using the tip of a sharp knife, check that the center of the meat is no longer pink and that the juices run clear. Cover in aluminum foil and let rest in a warm place for 30 minutes.

5. To make the sauce, mix together all of the ingredients in a small bowl. Set aside.

6. Boil or steam the sweet potatoes in a large saucepan until soft when pricked with the tip of a sharp knife. Drain and mash, then beat in the butter and pepper.

7. Remove any bones from the pork and pull the meat into large chunks. The meat should be tender, so this should not be hard to do. Put the pork into a large bowl and pour over the chili sauce. Gently mix, trying not to break up the pork too much.

8. Serve the pork with the mashed sweet potatoes.

1   4   5

Kale, Lemon & Chive Linguine

This tempting meat-free dish boasts a simple but fantastic fusion of fresh flavors, with the vibrant green of kale and chives adding to its appeal. Serve with a simple leaf salad and warm fresh crusty bread.

SERVES 2–3
Prepares in 15–20 minutes
Cooks in 20 minutes

9 ounces kale, thick stems removed, leaves sliced crosswise into thin ribbons (about 3¾ cups prepared)
8 ounces dried linguine
½ cup olive oil
1 onion, chopped
1 garlic clove, very thinly sliced
grated zest of 1 large lemon
large pinch of crushed red pepper flakes
3 tablespoons snipped fresh chives
¼ cup freshly grated Parmesan cheese
salt and pepper

1. Bring a large saucepan of water to a boil. Add the kale and blanch for 2 minutes, or until just wilted. Drain the kale, reserving the water, and set aside.

2. Return the reserved water to the saucepan and bring to a boil. Add the linguine and cook for 10–12 minutes, or according to the package directions, until tender but still firm to the bite.

3. Meanwhile, heat the oil in a large skillet over medium–high heat. Add the onion and sauté for 2–3 minutes, or until translucent. Add the garlic and sauté for an additional minute.

4. Stir in the kale, lemon zest, and crushed red pepper flakes, then season to taste with salt and pepper. Cook over medium heat for 4–5 minutes, stirring occasionally, until tender but still bright green. Add a little of the cooking water if the mixture becomes dry.

5. Drain the pasta and put into a warmed serving dish. Add the kale mixture, tossing with the pasta to mix. Stir in the chives and Parmesan with salt and pepper to taste. Toss again and serve immediately.

Seared Scallops with Fresh Mint & Red Chile Dressing

Prove your cooking prowess with this wonderful combination of seared fresh scallops served on a bed of peppery salad greens, with herb-filled lentils, crisp pan-fried pancetta, and a drizzle of mint and chile dressing.

SERVES 4–6
Prepares in 35 minutes
Cooks in 25–28 minutes

½ cup dried green lentils
2 garlic cloves
1 celery stalk
2 bay leaves
20 fresh parsley leaves, with stems
olive oil, for drizzling and frying
juice and zest of 1 lemon
2 tablespoons aged red wine vinegar
20 fresh basil leaves, coarsely chopped
20 fresh mint leaves, coarsely chopped
handful of arugula leaves, coarsely
  chopped
20 scallops
8 slices pancetta
salt and pepper
peppery salad greens, to serve

Mint & Red Chile Dressing
2 red chiles, seeded and chopped
small bunch of fresh mint, finely chopped
½ cup extra virgin olive oil
juice of 1 lemon
salt and pepper

1. Cover the lentils with cold water in a large saucepan and add the garlic, celery stalk, and bay leaves. Add a few parsley stems, bring to a boil, then reduce to a simmer.

2. Cook the lentil mixture for 12–15 minutes, or according to the package directions, until al dente and nutty. Taste them periodically so that they are not overcooked and soggy. Remove from the heat and drain off most of the water. Remove the garlic, bay leaves, celery stalk, and parsley stems. Season the lentils with olive oil, lemon juice and zest, some of the vinegar, and salt and pepper. Seasoning them when they are hot will help the lentils to absorb all the flavors.

3. When the lentils have cooled slightly, add the chopped herbs and arugula and stir until thoroughly combined. Set the lentils aside until ready to serve.

4. For the dressing, mix together the chiles and mint in a bowl with the olive oil and the lemon juice, and season with salt and pepper.

5. Clean the scallops by removing the small opaque muscle from the sides, then dry the scallops on paper towels. Add a tablespoon of oil to a skillet over high heat, add the slices of pancetta, and cook for about 2 minutes on each side, until crispy. Drain on paper towels.

6. Keep the skillet over high heat. Pat the scallops until dry and then season them with salt and pepper to taste. Add a splash more olive oil to the skillet.

7. Add the scallops and cook for 45 seconds. To turn the scallops, quickly use two tablespoons, one in each hand. Flick the scallops over from one spoon to the other.

8. Cook on the second side for about 40 seconds; when the scallops are caramelized on both sides, remove and place on clean paper towels.

9. Add a splash of vinegar to deglaze the skillet, then add the liquid to the dressing.

10. To serve, arrange some peppery salad greens on each plate and sprinkle the warm herb lentils over the top. Arrange some scallops on each plate and place the crisp pancetta on top. Spoon with some of the mint and chile dressing and serve immediately.

Wild Mushroom Risotto

Take your time to cook this classic recipe and your patience will be rewarded with an exquisitely creamy and flavorful mushroom risotto, perfect for a meat-free meal for sharing with friends at the weekend.

SERVES 6
Prepares in 20 minutes,
  plus soaking
Cooks in 30–40 minutes

2 ounces dried porcini mushrooms
about 1 pound mixed fresh
  wild mushrooms, such as portobello
  mushrooms and chanterelles,
  halved if large
¼ cup olive oil
3–4 garlic cloves, finely chopped
4 tablespoons butter
1 onion, finely chopped
2 cups risotto rice

¼ cup dry white vermouth
5 cups vegetable broth
1 cup freshly grated Parmesan cheese
¼ cup chopped fresh flat-leaf parsley
salt and pepper

1. Put the dried mushrooms into a heatproof bowl and add boiling water to cover. Set aside to soak for 30 minutes, then carefully lift out and pat dry. Strain the soaking liquid through a strainer lined with paper towels and set aside.

2. Trim the fresh mushrooms. Heat 3 tablespoons of the oil in a large skillet. Add the fresh mushrooms and sauté for 1–2 minutes. Add the garlic and the soaked mushrooms and cook, stirring frequently, for 2 minutes. Transfer to a plate.

3. Heat the remaining oil and half of the butter in a large, heavy saucepan. Add the onion and cook over medium heat, stirring occasionally, for 2 minutes, or until softened.

4. Reduce the heat, stir in the rice, and cook, stirring constantly, for 2–3 minutes, or until the grains are translucent. Add the vermouth and cook for 1 minute, until reduced.

5. Gradually add the hot broth, a ladleful at a time, until all the liquid is absorbed. Add half of the reserved mushroom soaking liquid to the risotto and stir in the mushrooms. Season to taste and add more mushroom liquid, if necessary. Stir in the remaining butter, grated Parmesan, and chopped parsley and serve.

Lobster Salad with Herb Mayonnaise

Flaunt your flair with this really impressive fresh lobster salad accompanied by homemade herb mayonnaise. Serve with potatoes and lettuce and you'll have created the ultimate salad of the season.

SERVES 4
Prepares in 40 minutes, plus freezing, cooling, and chilling
Cooks in 20 minutes

2 live lobsters, about 1¾ pounds, or 1 pound cooked fresh lobster meat
1 large cucumber
1 lettuce
4 hard-boiled eggs, halved
salt and pepper
steamed or boiled new potatoes and lettuce, to serve

Mayonnaise
2 egg yolks
1 teaspoon Dijon mustard
½ cup extra virgin olive oil
⅔ cup sunflower oil
1 tablespoon lemon juice
¼ cup cold water
small handful of fresh parsley, finely chopped
small handful of fresh dill, finely chopped
small handful of fresh chervil (optional), finely chopped
salt and pepper

1. If using fresh lobsters, put them into the freezer for 2 hours to kill them. Bring a large saucepan of heavily salted water to a boil and add the lobsters. Return to a boil and cook for 15 minutes. Remove from the heat, drain, and let cool.

2. To make the mayonnaise, combine the egg yolks and mustard in a food processor. Turn the processor on and, with the motor running, pour in the olive oil and then the sunflower oil in a slow, regular trickle, until the mixture has a good thick consistency. Add the lemon juice, water, and salt and pepper to taste and pulse again. Fold the herbs through, then put into a bowl and refrigerate until ready to use.

3. Peel, halve, and seed the cucumber. Cut into thin slivers, using a vegetable peeler.

4. Cut the lobster in half lengthwise, remove the dark vein that runs along the back of the tail, then remove the stomach sac that sits behind the mouth. Crack the claws with the back of a heavy knife.

5. Lay a bed of lettuce on each plate, sprinkle some cucumber over the leaves, then lay the egg halves and the halved lobsters on top. Season with salt and pepper, add the herb mayonnaise, and serve with potatoes and more lettuce.

Indian-Style Baked Fish in Banana Leaves

Wow your gathered guests with this simple but striking fish dish. Serve each diner their own sealed banana leaf package and enjoy their delight as they unwrap and discover a succulent, spicy fish fillet inside.

Look for coconut cream in larger supermarkets or Asian grocery stores, or scoop the cream from the top of canned coconut milk. (Don't mix up coconut cream with sweetened cream of coconut, used for making beverages.)

SERVES 4
Prepares in 25–30 minutes
Cooks in 15–20 minutes

4 thick cod fillets, about 7 ounces each, skinned
2 teaspoons ground turmeric
1 large fresh banana leaf

Spice Paste
2 teaspoons ground cumin
2 teaspoons ground coriander
1½ teaspoons palm or brown sugar
1 cup coconut cream
4 red chiles, seeded and chopped
2½ cups chopped fresh cilantro
¼ cup chopped fresh mint
5 garlic cloves, chopped
1 teaspoon finely grated fresh ginger
¼ cup vegetable or peanut oil
juice of 2 limes
2 teaspoons salt

1. Preheat the oven to 400°F.

2. Put the fish fillets in a single layer onto a plate and sprinkle with the turmeric. Rub into the fish and set aside.

3. Put the ingredients for the spice paste into a food processor and blend until fairly smooth. Set aside.

4. Cut the banana leaf into four 9½-inch squares. Soften the banana leaf squares by dipping them into a saucepan of hot water for a few seconds. Once they are pliant, wipe them dry with paper towels and arrange on a work surface.

5. Apply the spice paste liberally to both sides of each piece of fish. Place a piece of fish on top of each banana leaf square and wrap up like a package, securing with bamboo skewers or twine.

6. Put the packages into a baking pan and bake in the preheated oven for 15–20 minutes, or until cooked through. Transfer to plates and serve immediately.

Winning Wine Tips

Whether you are a wine connoisseur or a relative novice, when it comes to matching wine with food, there are no set rules, because it's often a matter of personal taste. However, some specific wines do pair well with certain foods, while other more versatile wines match with a wider variety of foods.

Many supermarkets, wine merchants, wine producers, and online warehouses offer expert advice, including recommendations on which wines are good partners for different foods. Wine labels (shelf and bottle labels) often include useful tips on this, too, or you may have your own long-standing favorites that will suit your meal perfectly.

Generally speaking, the most dominant ingredient or flavor in the dish you are serving is the one you want to match the wine with. You're aiming for a balance so that the wine and food complement each other and neither one overpowers the other.

For example, more delicate or light-flavored foods, such as simple chicken, white fish, pasta, or rice dishes, are often best when partnered with soft, lighter wines (primarily white wines, but some light red wines, too), whereas stronger, heartier dishes, such as beef, lamb, or steak recipes, tend to pair well with more flavorful medium or full-bodied red wines.

Some wines will easily span two or more courses (for example, an appetizer and main dish or a main dish and cheese and crackers), while others are best suited to just one course.

So, when matching wine with food, the main things to consider include the intensity of flavor and richness of the food, as well as the body or weight of the wine. The body and weight of the wine can be light, medium, or full-bodied (the alcohol level of the wine being the main contributor to the wine's body—alcohol gives wine its viscosity and consequent mouthfeel).

You should also consider the acidity of the wine (and the food), the tannins in the wine (tannins are most commonly found in red wines), and the sweetness of white wine (and the food).

It is important that you serve wine at the correct temperature to completely enjoy all the aromas and flavors at their best. Generally speaking, white, rose, and sparkling wines are best served chilled and red wines are better at room temperature, but there are exceptions to these rules and it's partly down to personal taste, too. Some lighter-bodied reds, for example, may be preferred slightly chilled. Check the label to see what is advised for the wine you are serving. A standard bottle of wine will serve around four to six people.

If you've chosen a red wine to go with your meal, be sure to let it breathe at room temperature before serving. You can do this by opening the bottle (and ideally pouring it into a wine decanter) about an hour or so before serving.

Make sure that white, rose, and sparkling wines are served well chilled. It could also be an idea to keep an ice bucket or wine chiller close on hand to keep the wine perfectly cold and to avoid having to go back and forth to the refrigerator during the meal. Make sure you keep a corkscrew handy as well, plus a wine bottle stopper or two to "recork" open bottles.

If the time is right to bring on the bubbles, there's no better way to set the tone for a special meal than by popping open a bottle of fizz. The three top choices are champagne from France, prosecco from Italy, or cava from Spain, although there are other interesting alternatives. Champagne is the premier fizz of the three, but also the priciest, with prosecco and cava offering good sparkling alternatives for those on a slightly less expensive budget.

For nonwine drinkers, chilled beers are good alternatives, as are cocktails. There are also nonalcoholic wines and beers for those who prefer not to drink alcohol or designated drivers. A pitcher of iced tap water or mineral water on the table is a welcome addition, too.

Roasted Fig Tarts with Crème de Cassis & Honey Mascarpone

Crème de cassis, or black currant syrup, and ripe fresh figs combine wonderfully on top of these crisp puff pastry tarts. Served with sumptuous honey mascarpone, these create the ideal indulgent desserts, guaranteed to satisfy all those with a sweet tooth.

SERVES 6
Prepares in 45–50 minutes,
  plus chilling

zest and juice of 1 orange

2 tablespoons honey

½ cup crème de cassis or
  black currant syrup

12 ripe black figs

flour, for dusting

1 (1-pound) package ready-to-bake
  puff pastry, thawed if frozen

1¼ sticks butter

¾ cup superfine or granulated sugar

1½ cups ground almonds (almond meal)

2 egg yolks

confectioners' sugar, for dusting

Honey Mascarpone

1¼ cups mascarpone cheese

2 tablespoons plain yogurt or
  crème fraîche

3 tablespoons honey

1 vanilla bean, halved and seeds removed

1. Preheat the oven to 350°F. In a small saucepan, mix the orange juice and honey and bring to a boil. Cook for about 10 minutes, or until reduced and syrupy, then add the crème de cassis. Halve the figs and put into the pan. Spoon the cassis mixture over the figs so they are well coated. Remove the pan from the heat.

2. Flour a board and roll out the pastry on the board to a thickness of ¼ inch. Using a saucer as a template, cut out six circles and place them on squares of parchment paper. Using a fork, prick plenty of holes in the center of the circles, leaving a clean border of ¾ inch around the edge of each circle. Place the circles in the refrigerator for 20 minutes, then transfer to the preheated oven and bake for 10 minutes.

3. Meanwhile, cream the butter and sugar in a food processor until smooth and pale, add the ground almonds and orange zest, and combine. Add the egg yolks and a tablespoon of the soaking juice from the figs, then mix until smooth.

4. When the pastry shells are a pale golden, spoon some of the almond mixture into the center of each. With the back of the spoon, spread the mixture up to the border, where the pastry will have risen more. Spoon four fig halves onto each tart and then spoon some of the cassis syrup on top.

5. Reduce the oven temperature to 325°F, transfer the tarts to the oven, and bake for 12 minutes, or until the mixture is set and the bottom of the pastry is crisp and golden brown. Reduce any leftover cassis liquid by simmering until thick and syrupy. Take the tarts out of the oven and spoon some of the hot syrup over the fruit.

6. To make the honey mascarpone, put the mascarpone cheese into a bowl and whisk together with the yogurt, honey, and the vanilla seeds. Whisk until smooth. Dust the tarts with confectioners' sugar and serve with the mascarpone.

Hot Chocolate Desserts & Candied Oranges

Chocolate and orange are a match made in heaven, especially in these mouthwatering molten-centered baked chocolate desserts served with candied oranges. For committed chocoholics, this decadent chocolate dessert will really hit the spot.

SERVES 6
Prepares in 55 minutes,
  plus cooling
Cooks in 1 hour 10 minutes

4½ ounces bittersweet chocolate,
  broken into pieces
6 tablespoons unsalted butter,
  plus extra for greasing
2 cloves
2 cardamom pods
¼ teaspoon ground cinnamon
¼ teaspoon ground nutmeg
zest of 1 large orange
2 extra-large eggs
2 extra-large egg yolks
3 tablespoons sugar
⅔ cup all-purpose flour,
  plus extra for dusting

Candied Orange Peel

5 oranges
2 cups water
8 cardamom pods
2 cinnamon sticks
2 cloves
½ teaspoon grated nutmeg
1½ cups sugar

1. Preheat the oven to 425°F. Lightly butter and flour six 2½-inch ramekins (individual ceramic dishes).

2. Put the chocolate and the butter into a heatproof bowl set over a saucepan of simmering water. Stir regularly to make sure it has an even texture.

3. In a mortar and pestle, crush the cloves with the cardamom pods, add the cinnamon and the nutmeg, then sift to a fine powder. When the chocolate is melted, remove from the heat and let cool. Stir in the ground spices and orange zest.

4. In a separate bowl, whisk the eggs, egg yolks, and the sugar until the eggs are pale and mousselike. Fold in the melted chocolate and the flour.

5. Pour the chocolate mixture into the prepared ramekins and bake in the preheated oven for 8–10 minutes. The centers of the desserts should be runny.

6. Meanwhile, make the candied orange peel. Remove the peel and pith of the oranges with a sharp knife. Cut into the flesh while doing this so that each piece consists of peel, pith, and about ¼ inch of flesh. You can eat the rest of the orange or save it for another dish.

7. While you are cutting the fruit, reserve the juice in a saucepan. Put the pieces of orange into the saucepan with the orange juice and cover with the water.

8. Bring to a simmer and let cook gently for 30 minutes, or until the liquid has reduced by one-third.

9. Using a mortar and pestle, crush the cardamom pods and discard the tough green shells. Add the seeds to the pan with the other spices and the sugar. Stir in the sugar to dissolve and then continue to boil the oranges for about 30 minutes. Let cool, then cut the peel into slivers and set aside until ready to serve. Reserve the syrup.

10. To serve, run a small blunt knife around the inside of each ramekin, gently turn out into the palm of your hand, and then plate on individual plates. Serve with the candied oranges and some of the reserved syrup.

Mocha Soufflés with Mascarpone

If you are looking to create a simple but sophisticated dinner party dessert, these individual towering baked soufflés are easy to make, but remember to serve them straight from the oven as soon as they are cooked.

SERVES 4
Prepares in 25–30 minutes,
  plus cooling
Cooks in 18–20 minutes

2 teaspoons butter, to grease
2 tablespoons ground almonds
1 tablespoon unsweetened cocoa powder,
   plus a little extra to dust
1 tablespoon strong espresso
small pinch of sea salt
⅓ cup cold water
3 egg whites
1 tablespoon rice malt syrup
¼ cup mascarpone cheese, to serve

1. Preheat the oven to 375°F. Lightly grease four ramekins (individual ceramic dishes), then sprinkle with the ground almonds. Roll and rotate the dishes so the almonds stick to the butter, coating all sides.

2. Put the cocoa powder, espresso, salt, and water into a small saucepan and cook, stirring, over low heat, until smooth. Increase the heat to medium–high and bring to a boil, then cook for an additional minute. Pour the mixture into a large bowl and let cool.

3. Put the egg whites into a separate large, clean mixing bowl and whisk until they form soft peaks. Add the rice malt syrup and whisk again until you have stiff peaks. Using a metal spoon, gently fold a spoonful of the egg white into the cocoa mixture, preserving as much air as possible, then fold in the rest.

4. Spoon the mixture into the ramekins. Bake in the preheated oven for 10–12 minutes, or until the soufflés are towering out of the ramekins.

5. Add a tablespoon of the mascarpone to each ramekin and sprinkle with the cocoa powder. Serve immediately, as quickly as possible before the soufflés start to collapse.

Spiced Plum & Blackberry Brûlées

These all-time favorite, rich and indulgent desserts are given a tempting twist with a wonderful mixture of lightly cooked fruits hidden beneath the luscious creamy layer on top. Perfect for a special seasonal sweet treat.

SERVES 6
Prepares in 25 minutes,
  plus cooling and chilling
Cooks in 14–15 minutes

4–5 plums (about 10½ ounces),
  pitted and sliced
1¼ cups blackberries
2 tablespoons water
¼ teaspoon ground cinnamon
⅓ cup firmly packed light brown sugar

1 cup heavy cream
1 cup Greek-style plain yogurt

1. Put the plums, blackberries, and water into a saucepan. Sprinkle with the cinnamon and 2 tablespoons of the sugar, then cover and cook over medium–low heat for 10 minutes, or until just tender. Let cool.

2. Put the cream into a large bowl and whisk until soft swirls form, then fold in the yogurt.

3. Spoon the fruit and a little of the juice from the pan into six ovenproof ¾-cup ramekins or soufflé dishes. Dot teaspoons of the cream mixture over the top, then spread it into an even layer. Chill for at least 30 minutes.

4. Preheat the broiler to high. Sprinkle the remaining sugar over the tops of the dishes. Stand them in the bottom of the broiler pan, pack ice around them to keep them cold, and broil for 4–5 minutes, or until the sugar has dissolved and caramelized. Let cool for 2 minutes, then serve immediately.

Goat Cheese with Honey & Walnuts

Goat cheese served simply with honey and walnuts makes a surprisingly appetizing combination, ideal for serving after a rich meal. For a fresh and fruity touch, add a few fresh pear slices to each serving, too.

SERVES 4
Prepares in 10–15 minutes
No cooking

about 6 ounces good-quality goat cheese, in one piece
about ½ cup honey, such as orange blossom or thyme-flavored
1 cup chopped walnuts

1. Remove the cheese from the refrigerator at least 20 minutes before serving to let it reach room temperature.

2. Pour the honey into a bowl. Put the walnuts into another bowl.

3. Serve the goat cheese on a cheese board with a cheese knife and let everyone cut a slice for themselves. Drizzle with some honey, with a dipper, if available, and sprinkle with chopped walnuts.

4. Alternatively, cut the cheese into quarters and place a slice on each of four serving plates. Drizzle with some honey, sprinkle with chopped nuts, and serve.

Champagne Sorbet

This elegant frozen dessert provides a really refreshing palate cleanser or luscious light dessert after an indulgent meal. Make it ahead of time, then simply soften it slightly and scoop when you are ready to serve.

SERVES 4
Prepares in 15–20 minutes,
  plus cooling and churning
  or freezing
Cooks in 5–7 minutes

juice of 1 lemon
1 cup water
¾ cup granulated sugar
1 tablespoon light corn syrup
1 cup champagne
mint leaves, to decorate

1. Combine all the ingredients except the champagne in a small saucepan. Put the saucepan over low heat and stir gently until all the sugar has dissolved. Increase the heat and bring to a boil, then remove from the heat. Let cool to room temperature.

2. When cooled, add the champagne and stir in. If using an ice cream maker, pour into the machine and churn for 30–45 minutes, or according to the manufacturer's directions.

3. Alternatively, freeze the mixture in a freezer-proof container, uncovered, for 1–2 hours, or until mushy. Turn the mixture into a bowl and stir vigorously to break down any ice crystals. Return the sorbet to the container and freeze for an additional 2–3 hours, or until firm. Cover the container with a lid for storing.

4. When ready to serve, let the sorbet soften slightly at room temperature before serving in sundae dishes, decorated with a few mint leaves.

Martini

Shaken, not stirred.

Champagne Sidecar

A great alternative to Mimosa.

Long Island Iced Tea

Classic and refreshing.

Black Velvet

For beer and wine lovers alike.

Martini

SERVES 1
Prepares in 10 minutes
No cooking

4–6 ice cubes, cracked
3 measures gin
1 teaspoon dry vermouth, or to taste
cocktail olive, to decorate

1. Put the cracked ice into a cocktail shaker.

2. Pour the gin and vermouth over the ice.

3. Shake until well frosted. Strain into a chilled cocktail glass.

4. Garnish with the olive. Serve immediately.

Champagne Sidecar

SERVES 1
Prepares in 10 minutes
No cooking

1½ measures bourbon
1 measure Cointreau
¼ measure lemon juice
ice
chilled champagne

1. Shake the bourbon, Cointreau, and lemon juice over ice and strain into a chilled flute.

2. Top up the flute with chilled champagne and serve immediately.

Long Island Iced Tea

SERVES 1
Prepares in 12 minutes
No cooking

cracked ice
1 measure vodka
1 measure gin
1 measure white tequila
1 measure white rum
½ measure white crème de menthe
2 measures lemon juice
1 teaspoon superfine sugar
cola
lime wedge, to decorate

1. Put cracked ice from 4–6 ice cubes into a cocktail shaker. Pour all the liquid ingredients except the cola over the ice, add the sugar, and shake vigorously until well frosted.

2. Fill a tall glass halfway with cracked ice and strain over the cocktail.

3. Top up with cola, garnish with the lime wedge, and serve immediately.

Black Velvet

SERVES 1
Prepares in 5 minutes
No cooking

stout, chilled
sparkling white wine, chilled

1. Fill a glass halfway with stout, then slowly pour in an equal quantity of wine over the back of a spoon that is just touching the top of the stout and the edge of the glass. Serve immediately.

Sunday All-Time Great Brunches

Sunday brunch is the perfect excuse to enjoy some tasty, laid-back food. This is the time for kicking back and relaxing as you enter the most chilled day of the weekend. Brunch food reflects this relaxed vibe, because it provides maximum enjoyment for a minimum of culinary effort. There's only one day left until work on Monday so make the most of it.

Sunday morning is all about lounging around and enjoying a long and lazy brunch. Once you get up, grind some fresh beans and get the coffee on, because nothing should be attempted before a leisurely cup of brewed joe. Then settle down with the papers for a while before starting to think about what delicious brunch dish you can throw together.

If you have a juicer or citrus press, you might want to squeeze some fresh fruit or vegetable juice and keep it chilled, ready to enjoy a little later, or bring out the blender and create a simple smoothie to boost your energy while you cook.

In this chapter, the focus is firmly on a wonderful selection of mouthwatering dishes, perfect for getting the taste buds going and all certain to deliver on flavor and appeal. These are relaxed and informal fuss-free meals that don't require too much effort, but that will satisfy those who enjoy something a little more substantial to start the day. We include flavor-packed egg scrambles, pancakes, platters, pies, tarts, and frittatas, all promising to hit the right spot on this most chilled-out of mornings.

Superb staples include Spinach Scrambled Eggs and Eggs Florentine, plus other delicious eats, such as Avocado, Bacon & Chile Frittata and Mini Salmon & Broccoli Pies. For vegetable lovers, the Vegetable Pancakes are sure to appeal to more adventurous eaters or those looking for something substantial to eat.

If you are in a celebratory mood or you are planning a really lazy afternoon, then why not try some tempting classic cocktail quenchers, such as Mint Julep or Bloody Mary, or the more decadent Champagne Cocktail.

Many of these recipes can be thrown together without much effort and some can be prepared ahead, too, making for easy eating on a Sunday morning. Depending on the number of guests

joining you for brunch, why not make a selection of dishes and let people just dig in and help themselves? The Whole-Wheat Spinach, Pea & Feta Tart and the Squash, Chorizo & Goat Cheese Quiche can both be made ahead. All that you will need to accompany these dishes is slices of fresh crusty bread or freshly made toast or some freshly baked croissants. Or, you could try some crispy crackers, a block of good-quality butter, and a jar or two of homemade relish or pickles.

On the other hand, if it's just a quiet weekend, why not indulge yourself and serve brunch in bed? It couldn't be easier to relax and while away the morning with this delicious selection of feel-good brunch favorites. What better way could there surely be to start your sleepy Sunday? The stresses of the working week could not be farther away.

Spinach Scrambled Eggs with Rye Toast

It's hard to beat scrambled eggs served with hot, crispy whole-grain toast for brunch, but lightly cooked spinach and a seasoning of nutmeg add extra flavor and appeal to this classic dish.

SERVES 4
Prepares in 15–20 minutes
Cooks in 9–12 minutes

1 (6-ounce) package spinach, chopped
8 extra-large eggs
3 tablespoons milk
1 tablespoon unsalted butter
4 slices of whole-grain rye bread
pinch of freshly grated nutmeg
salt and pepper

1. Put a large skillet over high heat. Add the spinach and cook in the water still clinging to it from washing, stirring for 1–2 minutes or until the leaves have just wilted. Transfer to a strainer and squeeze out as much of the moisture as possible. Keep warm.

2. Crack the eggs into a bowl, add the milk, and season with salt and pepper. Beat lightly with a fork until evenly mixed.

3. Melt the butter in the skillet over medium heat. Pour in the eggs and cook, stirring, for 5–6 minutes, or until they are just beginning to set. Add the spinach and cook, stirring, for 2–3 minutes, or until the eggs are lightly set.

4. Meanwhile, lightly toast the rye bread, then cut each slice in half.

5. Spoon the spinach scramble over the toast, sprinkle with nutmeg, and serve immediately.

1   2   4

Eggs Florentine

This superb egg-base staple is great for those who enjoy something a little more substantial to start the day. Serve it bubbling hot from the oven and dig in.

SERVES 4
Prepares in 15–20 minutes
Cooks in 15–20 minutes

1 tablespoon olive oil
1 (6-ounce) package baby spinach
4 thick slices ciabatta bread
2 tablespoons butter
4 extra-large eggs
1 cup shredded cheddar cheese
salt and pepper
freshly grated nutmeg, to serve

1. Preheat the broiler to high. Heat the oil in a wok or large saucepan, add the spinach, and sauté for 2–3 minutes, or until the leaves are wilted. Drain in a colander, season to taste with salt and pepper, and keep warm.

2. Toast the bread on both sides until golden. Spread one side of each slice with butter and place, buttered side up, in a baking dish.

3. Bring a small saucepan of lightly salted water to a boil, crack the eggs into the water, and poach for about 3 minutes, or until the whites are set but the yolks still runny. Remove from the pan with a slotted spoon.

4. Arrange the spinach on the toast and top each slice with a poached egg. Sprinkle with the shredded cheese. Cook under the preheated broiler for 1–2 minutes, until the cheese has melted. Sprinkle with nutmeg and serve immediately.

Zucchini Cakes with Smoked Salmon & Eggs

Individual pan-fried zucchini cakes, topped with thin slices of smoked salmon and creamy scrambled eggs makes a mouthwatering combination, creating the perfect choice for a lazy, leisurely Sunday brunch for two.

SERVES 2
Prepares in 25 minutes
Cooks in 12–16 minutes

3 extra-large eggs
1 tablespoon heavy cream
2 teaspoons finely snipped fresh chives
1 tablespoon butter
2 large slices of smoked salmon, to serve
salt and pepper

Zucchini Cakes

1 large zucchini, shredded
2 teaspoons quinoa flour
¼ cup freshly grated Parmesan cheese
1 extra-large egg yolk
1 tablespoon heavy cream
1 tablespoon vegetable oil

1. Preheat the oven to 225°F. To make the zucchini cakes, lay a clean dish towel on a work surface and pile the zucchini in the center. Holding the dish towel over the sink, gather the sides together, and twist them tightly until all the liquid from the zucchini has run out.

2. Put the zucchini, flour, Parmesan, egg yolk, and cream into a bowl and mix well. Roll the mixture into two balls and flatten them with the palms of your hands to make thick patties.

3. Heat the oil in a small skillet over medium–low heat. Cook the zucchini cakes for 5–8 minutes on each side, or until golden brown. Remove from the heat, transfer to a baking sheet, and put them in the oven to keep warm.

4. To make the scrambled eggs, crack the eggs into a bowl, add the cream and chives, and season with salt and pepper. Beat with a fork until evenly mixed.

5. Wipe the skillet clean with paper towels, then melt the butter in the pan over low heat. Pour in the egg mixture and cook, stirring, for 5–6 minutes, or until the eggs are just set.

6. Put the warm zucchini cakes on two plates. Spoon the scrambled eggs over them, then top with the salmon. Grind over some black pepper and serve immediately.

Yam, Rutabaga & Mushroom Hash

*For something that little
bit different, entice your
guests to the table with this
delicious pan-fried hash recipe
that uses yams—found in
Hispanic and Asian markets—
and rutabagas instead of
potatoes. Serve it straight
from the pan and all dig in.*

SERVES 4
Prepares in 20–25 minutes
Cooks in 25–30 minutes

3 tablespoons olive oil

3⅓ cups diced yams or sweet potatoes

*2 cups diced rutabaga, turnips,
   or butternut squash*

1 onion, chopped

6 ounces bacon, sliced or chopped

*4 cups sliced button mushrooms
   (about 8 ounces)*

4 eggs

salt and pepper

chopped fresh flat-leaf parsley, to garnish

1. Heat the oil in a large, lidded skillet over high heat. Add the yams and rutabagas to the pan, stir in the oil to coat, and season to taste generously with salt and pepper. Cook, stirring occasionally, for 10–15 minutes, or until all of the vegetables are just turning golden and soft.

2. Add the chopped onion and bacon to the skillet. Stir everything well and continue to cook for 5 minutes, or until the onion is soft and the bacon is cooked. Add the mushrooms to the pan, stir, and cover the pan. Cook the mixture for an additional 5 minutes.

3. Make four indentations in the mixture and carefully break an egg into each one. Cover the pan and cook for an additional 3–4 minutes, or until the egg whites are firm but the yolks are still soft.

4. Transfer the hash to four warm plates. Garnish each serving with the chopped parsley and serve immediately.

Antipasti Meat Platter

The simplicity of this dish is appealing—it looks great and everyone can just help themselves. Assemble the platter a little ahead of time if you prefer, then serve it when you are all ready to eat.

SERVES 4
Prepares in 20–25 minutes
No cooking

1 cantaloupe
2 ounces Italian salami, thinly sliced
8 slices prosciutto
8 slices bresaola
8 slices mortadella
4 plum tomatoes, thinly sliced
4 fresh figs, quartered

½ cup pitted black ripe olives
2 tablespoons shredded fresh basil
¼ cup extra virgin olive oil,
  plus extra to serve
pepper
sliced ciabatta loaf, to serve

1. Cut the melon in half, scoop out and discard the seeds, then cut the flesh into wedges. Arrange the wedges on one half of a large serving platter.

2. Arrange the salami, prosciutto, bresaola, and mortadella in loose folds on the other half of the platter. Arrange the tomato slices and fig quarters along the center of the platter.

3. Sprinkle the olives and basil over the platter and drizzle with oil. Season to taste with pepper, then serve with slices of ciabatta and extra oil, for dipping and drizzling.

Whole-Wheat Spinach, Pea & Feta Tart

A seasonal star of the summer kitchen, those opting for a meat-free day will savor the flavors of this tempting vegetable and feta cheese tart. Serve it simply with some peppery salad greens.

SERVES 6
Prepares in 35 minutes,
  plus chilling and cooling
Cooks in 1–1¼ hours

1 tablespoon unsalted butter
3 scallions, thinly sliced
1 (6-ounce) package baby spinach
⅔ cup shelled peas
3 eggs
1 cup milk
⅔ cup drained and finely
  crumbled feta cheese
¾ cup cherry tomatoes
salt and pepper

Pastry Dough
1 stick unsalted butter, cut into cubes
1¾ cups whole-wheat all-purpose flour,
  plus extra for dusting
2 eggs, beaten

1. To make the dough, put the butter and flour into a mixing bowl and season with salt and pepper. Rub the butter into the flour until it resembles fine crumbs. Gradually mix in enough egg to make a soft but not sticky dough.

2. Lightly dust a work surface with flour. Knead the dough gently, then roll it out on the surface to a little larger than a 10-inch loose-bottom tart pan. Lift the dough over the rolling pin, ease it into the pan, and press it into the sides. Trim the dough so that it stands a little above the top of the pan, then prick the bottom with a fork.

3. Cover the tart shell with plastic wrap and chill in the refrigerator for 15–30 minutes. Meanwhile, preheat the oven to 375°F.

4. To make the filling, melt the butter in a skillet over medium heat. Add the scallions and sauté for 2–3 minutes, or until softened. Add the spinach, turn the heat to high, and cook, stirring, until wilted. Set aside to cool.

5. Cook the peas in a small saucepan of boiling water for 2 minutes. Drain, then plunge into iced water and drain again. Crack the eggs into a small bowl, add the milk, season with salt and pepper, and beat with a fork.

6. Line the tart shell with parchment paper and pie weights or dried beans and place on a baking sheet. Bake for 10 minutes, then remove the paper and weights and bake for an additional 5 minutes, or until the bottom of the tart is crisp and dry.

7. Drain any cooking juices from the spinach mixture into the eggs. Put the mixture in the tart shell, add the peas, then sprinkle with the cheese. Fork the eggs and milk together once again, then pour into the tart shell and dot the tomatoes over the top. Bake for 40–50 minutes, or until set and golden. Let cool for 20 minutes, then serve.

Avocado, Bacon & Chile Frittata

An all-time favorite when it comes to brunch, frittatas are great for sharing. Avocados add an appealing taste twist and texture to this flavorful frittata, with fresh chile and lime juice adding a final touch of zing.

SERVES 4
Prepares in 20–25 minutes
Cooks in 12–17 minutes

1 tablespoon vegetable oil
8 bacon strips, coarsely chopped
6 eggs, beaten
3 tablespoons heavy cream
2 large avocados, sliced
1 red chile, seeded and thinly sliced
½ lime
salt and pepper

1. Preheat the broiler to medium. Heat the oil in an 8-inch ovenproof skillet over medium heat. Add the bacon and cook, stirring, for 4–5 minutes, or until crisp and golden. Using a slotted spoon, transfer to a plate lined with paper towels. Remove the pan from the heat.

2. Pour the eggs into a bowl, add the cream, and season with salt and pepper, then beat. Return the pan to the heat. When it is hot, pour in the egg mixture and cook for 1–2 minutes, without stirring. Sprinkle the bacon and avocado on top and cook for an additional 2–3 minutes, or until the frittata is almost set and the underside is golden brown.

3. Put the frittata under the broiler and cook for 3–4 minutes, or until the top is golden brown and the egg is set. Sprinkle with the chile and squeeze with the lime juice. Cut into wedges and serve.

Vegetable Pancakes with Pesto & Braised Spinach

Homemade pesto is hard to beat and it is wonderful combined with the white sauce and braised spinach in this recipe. Served with crisply cooked homemade pancakes, this is sure to be a hit with any guests.

SERVES 6
Prepares in 50 minutes,
 plus cooling
Cooks in 50–55 minutes

1 cup store-bought white sauce
 (for homemade, see page 163, Step 2)
olive oil, for frying
arugula, to serve

Pancake Batter
2⅓ cups all-purpose flour
2 egg yolks
2 tablespoons olive oil
2 cups milk
salt and pepper

Pesto
3 tablespoons pine nuts
2 large garlic cloves
½ teaspoon coarse salt

2 bunches of fresh basil
¾ cup freshly grated Parmesan cheese
½ cup olive oil
juice of ½ lemon

Braised Spinach
1 tablespoon extra virgin olive oil
1 garlic clove,
 finely sliced lengthwise
1 (10-ounce) package baby spinach
a splash of lemon juice
salt and pepper

1. Preheat the oven to 375°F. For the pesto, roast the pine nuts on a baking sheet for 3–4 minutes, or until golden brown. Crush the garlic with the salt, using the side of a heavy knife. Using a mortar and pestle, crush the garlic and the pine nuts to a coarse paste. Coarsely chop the basil and then add to the mortar and pestle, a handful at a time. Continue to pound until you have a smooth paste, then stir in the grated Parmesan cheese.

2. Gradually add the olive oil and the lemon juice and season with salt and pepper. Use immediately or store in an airtight container in the refrigerator.

3. For the spinach, heat the olive oil in a large, heavy saucepan or wok. Sauté the garlic until it is pale golden. Add all the spinach to the hot oil. Cover with a lid and cook for about 2 minutes, or until the leaves are wilted. Shake well and remove the lid. Stir to make sure all the leaves are wilted. Drain off any excess water and liquid. Season with salt and pepper, and a splash of lemon juice. Mix together.

4. Mix the pesto with the white sauce and then stir into the spinach. Adjust the seasoning.

5. To make the pancake batter, sift the flour into a large bowl and make a well in the center. Place the egg yolks in the well. Add some salt and pepper and the olive oil. Whisk together until everything is thoroughly combined. Whisk in the milk until you have a smooth batter.

6. Heat a nonstick skillet or an omelet pan. When hot, add a little olive oil, then pour out the excess. Use a ladle to pour some batter into the hot pan. Lift the pan and move it around so the batter covers the bottom of the pan. Pour the excess batter back into the bowl.

7. Cook the pancake over medium–high heat for 1–2 minutes, or until the underside is crisp and golden brown. Using a spatula, turn the pancake and cook on the other side. When completely cooked, remove the pancake from the pan and let cool on some paper towels to soak up any oil. Repeat the process, making pancakes and leaving them to cool on the paper, until all the batter has been used. Preheat the oven to 350°F.

8. When the pancakes have cooled, lay them out and spread the pesto-and-spinach mixture in a thick dollop in the center of the pancakes. Fold in the two sides and then roll them into a cylinder.

9. Arrange the stuffed pancakes in an ovenproof dish, put into the preheated oven, and bake for 8–10 minutes. Serve the pancakes immediately, with the arugula on the side.

Squash, Chorizo & Goat Cheese Quiche

Roasted butternut squash and spicy chorizo team up in this creamy baked quiche that is sure to get taste buds going as the delicious aromas waft from the oven. This is an excellent brunch dish for sharing.

SERVES 4
Prepares in 35 minutes,
  plus chilling and cooling
Cooks in 1 hour 20 minutes

3 cups diced butternut squash

1 tablespoon olive oil

7 ounces chorizo, cut into
  small, irregular chunks

3 eggs

½ cup crème fraîche or sour cream

2 tablespoons fresh thyme leaves

4 ounces semihard goat cheese

salt and pepper

salad greens, to serve (optional)

Pastry Dough

4 tablespoons cold butter, diced

¾ cup whole-wheat flour,
  plus extra for dusting

2 tablespoons cold water

1. Preheat the oven to 375°F.

2. To make the dough, put the butter into a mixing bowl, add the flour, and season with salt and pepper. Rub the butter into the flour until it resembles fine bread crumbs. Alternatively, process it in a food processor. Gradually mix in enough of the water to make a soft, but not sticky, dough.

3. Lightly dust a work surface with flour. Pat the dough into a circle, then wrap it tightly in plastic wrap. Chill in the refrigerator for at least 30 minutes.

4. Meanwhile, to make the filling, put the butternut squash and oil into a large roasting pan, season with salt and pepper, and toss well.

5. Roast in the preheated oven for 15 minutes, then stir and add the chorizo. Roast for an additional 15 minutes, or until the squash is crisp on the edges and tender, and the chorizo is crisp. Set aside to cool.

6. Dust the work surface with more flour. Knead the dough gently, then roll it out to a circle that is just under 9 inches in diameter. Place on a baking sheet and prick all over with a fork.

7. Bake in the preheated oven for 20 minutes. Remove from the oven and, using the bottom of an 8-inch loose-bottom tart pan as a template, cut a circle in the pastry. Set aside to cool.

8. Meanwhile, crack the eggs into a large bowl and lightly beat with a fork. Stir in the crème fraîche and thyme and season with plenty of pepper.

9. Reduce the oven temperature to 325°F. Line the 8-inch tart pan with parchment paper.

10. Carefully place your cooled pastry circle in the pan, then sprinkle with the chorizo and butternut squash. Pour the egg mixture over them, then crumble the goat cheese on top.

11. Bake the quiche in the preheated oven for 30 minutes, or until the egg in the center is set.

12. Serve the quiche warm or at room temperature and with salad greens on the side, if using.

Mini Salmon & Broccoli Pies

Show off your pastry-making skills with these ultimate individual golden baked pies. These tasty treats are perfect for Sunday brunch with friends.

MAKES 8
Prepares in 35 minutes,
 plus cooling and chilling
Cooks in 40–45 minutes

Filling

1¾ cups broccoli florets
4½ ounces salmon fillet
2 tablespoons butter
3 tablespoons all-purpose flour
1 cup warm milk
salt and pepper
salad, to serve

Pastry Dough

1¾ cups all-purpose flour,
 plus extra for dusting
pinch of salt
1 stick butter
about 3 tablespoons iced water
1 egg, lightly beaten with
 1 tablespoon water

1. Cook the broccoli in lightly salted boiling water for 5–10 minutes, or until tender. Drain and let cool. Meanwhile, bring a saucepan of lightly salted water to a boil, then reduce the heat to low. Add the fish and poach, turning once, for 5 minutes, or until the flesh flakes easily. Remove from the pan and let cool.

2. To make a white sauce, melt the butter in a small saucepan, add the flour, and cook over low heat, stirring constantly, for 2 minutes. Gradually stir in the warm milk. Bring to a boil, stirring constantly, then simmer, stirring, until thickened and smooth. Season to taste, remove from the heat, and let cool, stirring occasionally.

3. Meanwhile, to make the dough, sift the flour and salt into a bowl. Add the butter and cut into the flour. Rub in with your fingertips until the mixture resembles bread crumbs. Stir in the water and mix to a smooth dough.

4. Shape the dough into a ball, cover, and chill for 30 minutes.

5. Remove the skin and flake the flesh of the fish into a bowl. Break up the broccoli florets and add to the bowl. Stir in the white sauce and season to taste. Mix well.

6. Preheat the oven to 400°F. Roll out the dough on a lightly floured surface and stamp out 16 circles with a 4-inch cutter. Put eight circles into a muffin pan. Add spoonfuls of the salmon mixture without filling the pastry shells completely. Brush the edges of the remaining circles with water and use to cover the pies, pressing with the tines of a fork to seal.

7. Brush the tops with the beaten egg mixture and bake for 20–25 minutes, or until golden brown. Serve with salad.

Fresh Lemonade
Perfect on a summer's morning.

Champagne Cocktail
A relaxing start to a Sunday.

Mint Julep
A refreshing cocktail for a brunch with friends.

Bloody Mary
The ultimate brunch companion.

Fresh Lemonade

SERVES 6
Prepares in 20 minutes, plus standing
No cooking

4 large lemons, preferably unwaxed
¾ cup sugar
3½ cups boiling water
ice cubes

1. Scrub the lemons well, then dry. Using a vegetable peeler, peel three of the lemons thinly. Put the peel into a small bowl, add the sugar and boiling water, and stir well until the sugar has dissolved. Cover the small bowl and let stand for at least 3 hours, stirring occasionally. Meanwhile, squeeze the juice from the 3 lemons and reserve.

2. Remove and discard the lemon peel and stir in the reserved lemon juice. Thinly slice the remaining lemon and cut the slices in half. Add to the lemonade together with the ice cubes. Stir and serve immediately.

Champagne Cocktail

SERVES 1
Prepares in 10 minutes
No cooking

1 sugar cube
2 dashes Angostura bitters
1 measure brandy
champagne, chilled

1. Place the sugar cube in the bottom of a chilled flute. Add the bitters and the brandy.

2. Top up with champagne and serve immediately.

Mint Julep

SERVES 1
Prepares in 10 minutes
No cooking

1 fresh mint sprig, plus extra to decorate
1 tablespoon sugar syrup
cracked ice
3 measures bourbon

1. Strip the leaves from the mint sprig and put into a small chilled glass.

2. Crush the mint leaves and pour in the sugar syrup.

3. Fill the glass halfway with cracked ice and stir. Add the bourbon and decorate with the remaining mint sprig. Serve immediately.

Bloody Mary

SERVES 1
Prepares in 10 minutes
No cooking

4–6 ice cubes, cracked
dash hot pepper sauce
dash Worcestershire sauce
2 measures vodka
6 measures tomato juice
juice of ½ lemon
pinch celery salt
pinch cayenne pepper
celery stalk and lemon slice, to decorate

1. Put the ice into a cocktail shaker. Dash the hot pepper sauce and Worcestershire sauce over the ice.

2. Add the vodka, tomato, and lemon juices and shake vigorously. Strain into a tall glass, add the celery salt and cayenne, and decorate with the celery and lemon.

Sunday
Long & Lazy
Lunches

Sunday is the ideal time over the weekend to invite friends or family around and enjoy a long and lazy lunch together. This chapter is all about creating delicious dishes that really pack a flavor punch, without being complicated or fastidious. Be it for a special occasion, a celebratory meal, or simply an excuse for a culinary blowout, these meals provide the perfect opportunity to gather guests around the table and tempt them with some superb standout dishes.

Sunday morning often affords you a little more scope in the kitchen, making it the prime time to prepare a feast of flavors for your companions. Long, slow roasts, in particular, lend themselves to Sunday lunch dining, because you can take your time to make the meal while talking with friends as you cook. Delicious dishes that need a little more attention during cooking, such as paellas and stews, are ideal for Sunday lunch entertaining, too, allowing you to get the best out of the food you love to prepare.

To whet the appetite, kick things off with a tasty array of assorted small bites to nibble on and to accompany a selection of chilled beverages or aperitifs. Once your guests are relaxed and ready to eat, select a simple but stylish appetizer that everyone can dig into, such as prosciutto and fresh figs, blinis with smoked salmon, a tasty pâté, or a beautiful baked camembert cheese, but make sure you leave plenty of room for the main event.

Next up, it's time to show off your culinary prowess and wow your guests with a magnificent main dish. We feature an appealing collection of full-on-flavor dishes, including roasts, grills, tarts, and stews. For those who prefer a meaty meal, you can opt for the taste of beef with Standing Rib Roast with Roasted Potatoes & Popovers or try Pork Chops with Applesauce. Or for a twist on a classic, try Cornish Game Hens Stuffed with Spiced Sour Cherries. For fish lovers, we include the perfect Spanish Paella, as well as a more contemporary Fish Stew with Cider, and then for those who prefer a vibrant vegetable-base option, the appetizing Asparagus Tart is sure to be a winner.

Baked, braised, grilled, glazed, or roasted vegetables will all provide tempting sides to both traditional and more contemporary dishes, or you can go for a slightly more sophisticated side, such as Roasted Root Vegetables.

To satisfy those with a sweet tooth, it's time to perfect your dessert skills and finish the meal with a little gourmet flair. All-time prize picks include a billowing Apple Pie or Maple & Pecan Pie, but if you prefer a decadent chocolate dessert, Brownie Sundae will be a real treat. A decent dollop of whipped cream or crème fraîche, a scoop or two of luscious ice cream, or a generous drizzle of cream or hot, creamy custard, will provide the perfect accompaniment.

2   2   3

Pork Chops with Applesauce

A fuss-free favorite, these succulent pork chops, served with a mildly spiced, homemade applesauce, guarantee comfort food at its best. Serve with roasted potatoes and a selection of seasonal fresh vegetables for the perfect Sunday lunch.

SERVES 4
Prepares in 20–25 minutes
Cooks in 25–30 minutes,
  plus standing

4 pork rib chops on the bone,
  each about 1¼ inches thick,
  at room temperature
1½ tablespoons sunflower oil or canola oil
salt and pepper

Applesauce
3 cooking apples, such as Granny Smiths
  (about 1 pound), peeled, cored,
  and diced
¼ cup sugar, plus extra, if needed
finely grated zest of ½ lemon
1½ teaspoons lemon juice,
  plus extra, if needed
¼ cup water
¼ teaspoon ground cinnamon
pat of butter

1. Preheat the oven to 400°F.

2. To make the applesauce, put the apples, sugar, lemon zest, lemon juice, and water into a heavy saucepan over high heat and bring to a boil, stirring, to dissolve the sugar. Reduce the heat to low, cover, and simmer for 15–20 minutes, or until the apples are tender and fall apart when you mash them against the side of the pan. Stir in the cinnamon and butter and beat the apples until they are as smooth or chunky as you prefer. Stir in extra sugar or lemon juice to taste. Remove the pan from the heat, cover, and keep the applesauce warm.

3. Meanwhile, pat the chops dry and season to taste with salt and pepper. Heat the oil in a large ovenproof skillet over medium–high heat. Add the chops and cook for 3 minutes on each side to brown.

4. Transfer the pan to the oven and roast the chops for 7–9 minutes, until cooked through and the juices run clear when you cut into the chops. Remove the pan from the oven, cover with aluminum foil, and let stand for 3 minutes. Gently reheat the applesauce, if necessary.

5. Transfer the chops to warm plates and spoon over the pan juices. Serve immediately, accompanied by the applesauce.

Cornish Game Hens Stuffed with Spiced Sour Cherries

For a truly tasty twist on a classic, try these sophisticated stuffed roasted birds. Served on a large platter to impress, everyone then gets to enjoy their own whole bird, sprinkled with a splendid spiced fruit-nut mixture.

SERVES 4
Prepares in 35–40 minutes
Cooks in 35–45 minutes

3 garlic cloves, finely chopped
1 red chile, seeded
    and finely chopped
3 onions, finely sliced
2 tablespoons coriander seeds
2 teaspoons ground cinnamon
2 teaspoons ground allspice
juice and zest of 2 lemons
4 bay leaves

⅔ cup dried sour cherries
⅔ cup dried cranberries
⅔ cup pistachio nuts
2 tablespoons extra virgin olive oil, plus
    extra for frying and drizzling
4 Cornish game hens
salt and pepper
roasted potatoes or a salad
    of peppery leaves, to serve

1. Preheat the oven to 350°F. Mix the garlic and chile with the onions. Use a mortar and pestle to crush the coriander seeds, then add to the garlic-and-onion mixture with the other ground spices. Add the lemon juice and zest and the bay leaves and mix everything together in a bowl with the dried fruits and nuts. Add the oil, mix well, and season with salt and pepper.

2. Stuff each hen with a generous amount of the stuffing. Heat a little oil in a Dutch oven or a heavy flameproof casserole dish. Season the hens on the outside with salt and pepper.

3. Put the hens into the Dutch oven and brown both breasts and the back. Transfer the Dutch oven to the preheated oven.

4. Roast the hens in the preheated oven for 30–35 minutes, or until the meat is tender, basting regularly with all the roasting juices. To check that the meat is ready, insert the tip of a small knife into the thickest part of the meat—check that there is no trace of pink and the juices run clear.

5. To serve, spoon the stuffing out of the hens and sprinkle it over the top of the birds. Drizzle with some olive oil to add an attractive shine. Serve the hens on a large platter surrounded by roasted potatoes or with a fresh salad of bitter and peppery leaves.

Standing Rib Roast with Roasted Potatoes & Popovers

For a truly standout traditional roast beef, standing rib roast served with all the trimmings creates a popular Sunday lunch meal that is great for celebrating a special occasion with a family group or friends.

SERVES 8
Prepares in 40 minutes
Cooks in 2 hours 10 minutes, plus resting

olive oil, for rubbing
6½-pound standing rib roast
½ tablespoon all-purpose flour
1 cup beef broth
1 cup red wine
salt and pepper

Popovers
2 cups all-purpose flour, sifted
6 eggs
½ teaspoon salt
2½ cups milk
2 tablespoons vegetable oil or lard

Roasted Potatoes
4½ pounds Bintje or new potatoes, halved if large
⅓ cup sunflower oil, goose fat, or duck fat
salt and pepper

To Serve
roasted carrots
steamed broccoli
horseradish sauce (optional)
mustard (optional)

1. For the popovers, mix the flour, eggs, and salt together in a bowl, then gradually add the milk as you stir with a whisk. When smooth, set aside but do not chill.

2. Meanwhile, preheat the oven to 425°F.

3. Rub a generous amount of olive oil and salt and pepper into the beef, then put into a roasting pan. Transfer to the preheated oven and roast for 30 minutes.

4. For the roasted potatoes, bring a large saucepan of lightly salted water to a boil, add the potatoes, bring back to a boil, and cook for 10 minutes. Drain the potatoes and toss them in oil and salt and pepper. Put them into a roasting pan in a single layer.

5. Reduce the temperature to 325°F. Transfer the potatoes to the oven and roast with the beef for 1 hour.

6. Remove the beef from the oven and increase the oven temperature to 425°F. Cover the beef with aluminum foil and let rest for at least 30 minutes.

7. Keep the potatoes in the oven. Put a 16 x 10-inch roasting pan in the bottom of the oven to warm for the popover mixture.

8. To cook the popovers, remove the roasting pan from the bottom of the oven and add the vegetable oil. Put it back in the oven for 5 minutes, then remove the pan and add the popover batter to the bottom of the pan. Put it back in the hot oven for about 20 minutes.

9. Meanwhile, make the gravy. Remove the beef from the pan and stir the flour into the leftover juices, add the broth and wine, then simmer over medium heat until reduced by about half.

10. Remove the popover from the oven and divide it into eight pieces. Then remove the potatoes from the oven. Cut the rib bones off the meat and carve the beef.

11. Serve the beef with the potatoes, popovers, carrots, broccoli, gravy, and horseradish sauce and mustard, if desired.

Grilled & Marinated Loin of Lamb

These marvelous marinated lamb loin roasts are grilled, then baked to perfection and served with a delicious potato and mushroom medley to make this tempting Sunday lunch.

SERVES 4
Prepares in 45 minutes,
  plus marinating
Cooks in 35–40 minutes,
  plus resting

2¼ pounds new potatoes,
  scrubbed or peeled
3 tablespoons olive oil
9 ounces mixed portobello
  and wild mushrooms
2 garlic cloves, finely chopped
1 tablespoon chopped fresh thyme
juice of 1 lemon
1 small handful of fresh flat-leaf parsley,
  coarsely chopped
salt and pepper
fresh pesto, to serve

Lamb

2 boneless single lamb loin roasts,
  10–12 ounces each, trimmed
4 garlic cloves, coarsely crushed
2 tablespoons chopped fresh rosemary
juice and zest of 1 lemon
3 tablespoons olive oil

1. For the lamb, make cuts into the surfaces of the roasts. Mix the garlic and rosemary with some pepper in a bowl, then rub the mixture into the cut surfaces of the meat. Put the roasts into a shallow dish and add the lemon juice and zest and the olive oil. Turn over the meat a couple of times to make sure the roasts are coated, then cover. Let marinate at room temperature for at least 2 hours, turning occasionally.

2. Preheat the oven to 400°F.

3. Cut the potatoes into ¼-inch slices. Toss with 2 tablespoons of olive oil and some salt and pepper. Put into a baking pan in a single layer and cook for about 15 minutes.

4. Meanwhile, clean the mushrooms with a small knife or brush, or a damp cloth. Do not wash. Tear into even strips. In a heavy saucepan, heat the remaining oil and sauté the garlic and thyme until pale golden. Add the mushrooms and cook over high heat, stirring regularly.

5. Cook off all the watery liquid. If you are using a small saucepan, you might want to divide the garlic and thyme in two and sauté the mushrooms in smaller batches to avoid overcrowding the pan. Sauté the mushrooms for 3–4 minutes. Season with salt and pepper, add the lemon juice, and cook for an additional minute.

6. When the potatoes are two-thirds cooked and are beginning to crisp around the edges, add the mushrooms to the baking pan and mix together. Set aside and do not put back in the oven yet.

7. Preheat a ridged grill pan over high heat. Remove the meat from the marinade and pat dry. Season with salt and a little pepper.

8. Place the roasts directly on the grill pan and seal for 2 minutes on each side, then remove and place on top of the potatoes and mushrooms. Return the baking pan to the oven and roast for 15–20 minutes, until the lamb is cooked through or to your preference.

9. Remove the baking pan from the oven and sprinkle with the chopped parsley. Let the meat rest for a couple of minutes before serving.

10. Slice the lamb into thick slices. Plate up the potatoes and mushrooms on each plate, then add the lamb and finish with plenty of the bright green pesto splashed on top.

Asparagus Tart

Bake this seasonal gem in late spring or early summer and enjoy tender, fresh asparagus spears at their best. This tasty tart is great for alfresco lunchtime dining in warm weather, with a glass of chilled white wine.

SERVES 4
Prepares in 30–35 minutes, plus cooling
Cooks in 55 minutes–1 hour 5 minutes

1 (1-pound) package rolled dough pie crust, chilled
butter, for greasing
all-purpose flour, for dusting
1 bunch thin asparagus spears
1 (10-ounce) package baby spinach
3 extra-large eggs, beaten
⅔ cup heavy cream
1 garlic clove, crushed
10 small cherry tomatoes, halved
handful of chopped fresh basil
¼ cup grated Parmesan cheese
salt and pepper

1. Preheat the oven to 375°F. Remove the dough from the refrigerator at least 15 minutes before use, otherwise it may be brittle and difficult to handle.

2. Grease a 10-inch tart pan with butter, then roll out the dough on a lightly floured surface and line the pan with it. Cut off any excess dough, prick the bottom with a fork, cover with a piece of parchment paper, and fill with pie weights or dried beans. Bake in the preheated oven for 20–30 minutes, or until lightly browned.

3. Take the tart shell out of the oven, remove the parchment paper and weights, and let cool slightly. Reduce the oven temperature to 350°F.

4. Meanwhile, bend the asparagus spears until they snap, and discard the woody bottoms.

5. Bring a large saucepan of water to a boil, add the asparagus, and blanch for 1 minute, then remove and drain. Add the spinach to the boiling water, then remove immediately and drain well.

6. Mix the eggs, cream, and garlic together in a small bowl and season to taste with salt and pepper.

7. Lay the blanched spinach along the bottom of the tart shell, add the asparagus and tomatoes, cut side up, sprinkle with the basil, then pour the egg mixture on top.

8. Transfer to the preheated oven and bake for about 35 minutes, or until the filling has just set. Sprinkle the Parmesan cheese on top and let cool to room temperature before serving or serve immediately.

Chicken, Chorizo & Seafood Paella

Take your time to prepare the perfect paella and impress your guests with this popular full-on-flavor rice dish. It's packed with chicken, chorizo, vegetables, rice, and seafood, creating a complete meal that's great for feeding a crowd.

SERVES 6–8
Prepares in 35–40 minutes,
  plus soaking
Cooks in 50–55 minutes

⅓ cup olive oil
6–8 boned chicken thighs
5 ounces chorizo, diced
2 large onions, chopped
4 large garlic cloves, crushed
1 teaspoon mild or hot paprika
2 cups Spanish or medium-grain rice,
  rinsed and drained
1 cup chopped green beans
1 cup frozen peas
5½ cups fish broth

½ teaspoon saffron threads, soaked in
  2 tablespoons hot water
16 mussels, scrubbed, debearded, and
  soaked in salted water for 10 minutes
16 shrimp, peeled and deveined
2 red bell peppers, halved and seeded,
  then broiled, peeled, and sliced
salt and pepper
chopped fresh parsley, to garnish

1. Heat 3 tablespoons of the olive oil in a 12-inch paella pan or casserole dish. Add the chicken to the casserole and cook over medium–high heat, turning frequently, for 5 minutes, or until golden and crisp.

2. Using a slotted spoon, transfer the chicken to a bowl.

3. Add the chorizo to the casserole dish and cook, stirring, for 1 minute, or until beginning to crisp, then add to the chicken.

4. Heat the remaining oil in the pan, add the onions, and sauté, stirring, for 2 minutes. Add the garlic and paprika and sauté for an additional 3 minutes, or until the onions are softened but not brown.

5. Add the rice, beans, and peas and stir until coated in oil. Return the chicken and chorizo and any accumulated juices to the pan. Stir in the broth, saffron and its soaking liquid, and salt and pepper to taste and bring to a boil, stirring. Reduce the heat to low and simmer, uncovered, for 15 minutes.

6. Discard any mussels with broken shells and any that refuse to close when tapped. Arrange the mussels, shrimp, and roasted peppers on top. Cover and simmer for 5 minutes, until the shrimp turn pink and the mussels open. Discard any mussels that remain closed. Make sure the chicken is cooked through and the juices run clear by piercing the thickest part of the meat with the tip of a sharp knife.

7. Garnish with the parsley and serve immediately.

Fish Stew with Cider

For a contemporary change to a fishy favorite, try this fantastic fish stew that has an intriguing addition of hard cider in the creamy sorrel sauce. It's a good way to showcase sustainable fresh fish, such as monkfish or cod.

SERVES 4
Prepares in 30 minutes
Cooks in 40–45 minutes

2 teaspoons butter
1 large leek, thinly sliced
2 shallots, finely chopped
½ cup hard dry cider or apple juice
1¼ cups fish broth
2 Yukon gold potatoes, diced
1 bay leaf

¼ cup all-purpose flour
1 cup milk
1 cup heavy cream
2 cups chopped fresh sorrel leaves
12 ounces skinless monkfish or cod
  fillet, cut into 1-inch pieces
salt and pepper

1. Melt the butter in a large saucepan over medium–low heat. Add the leek and shallots and cook for about 5 minutes, stirring frequently, until they start to soften. Add the cider and bring to a boil.

2. Stir in the broth, potatoes, and bay leaf with a large pinch of salt (unless the broth is salty) and bring back to a boil. Reduce the heat, cover, and cook gently for 10 minutes.

3. Put the flour into a small bowl and slowly whisk in a few tablespoons of the milk to make a thick paste. Stir in a little more milk to make a smooth liquid.

4. Adjust the heat so the stew bubbles gently. Stir in the flour mixture and cook, stirring frequently, for 5 minutes. Add the remaining milk and half of the cream. Continue cooking for about 10 minutes, or until the potatoes are tender. Remove and discard the bay leaf.

5. Combine the sorrel with the remaining cream. Stir the sorrel cream into the stew and add the fish. Continue cooking, stirring occasionally, for about 3 minutes, or until the monkfish stiffens. Taste the stew and adjust the seasoning, if needed. Ladle into serving bowls and serve.

Roasted Root Vegetables

SERVES 4–6

Prepares in 25 minutes, plus optional marinating

Cooks in 50–60 minutes

3 parsnips, cut into 2-inch chunks

4 baby turnips, cut into quarters

3 carrots, cut into 2-inch chunks

½ butternut squash, cut into 2-inch chunks

3 sweet potatoes, cut into 2-inch chunks

2 garlic cloves, finely chopped

2 tablespoons chopped fresh rosemary

2 tablespoons chopped fresh thyme

2 teaspoons chopped fresh sage

3 tablespoons olive oil

salt and pepper

2 tablespoons chopped fresh mixed herbs, such as parsley, thyme, and mint, to garnish

1. Preheat the oven to 425°F.

2. Arrange all the vegetables in a single layer in a large roasting pan. Sprinkle with the garlic, rosemary, thyme, and sage. Pour the oil over the vegetables and season well with salt and pepper.

3. Toss all the ingredients together until they are well mixed and coated with the oil (you can leave them to marinate at this stage to let the flavors be absorbed).

4. Roast the vegetables at the top of the preheated oven for 50–60 minutes, or until they are cooked and nicely browned. Turn the vegetables over halfway through the cooking time.

5. Serve immediately, garnished with the mixed herbs.

Steamed Greens with Lemon & Cilantro

SERVES 4
Prepares in 15 minutes
Cooks in 6 minutes

*1 head of cabbage, tough outer
leaves discarded*
1 (6-ounce) package baby spinach
large pat of unsalted butter
finely grated zest of ½ lemon
¼ cup chopped fresh cilantro
salt and pepper

1. Cut the cabbage in quarters lengthwise and cut out the tough core. Slice the quarters crosswise into ¾-inch ribbons. Steam for 3 minutes, or until starting to soften.

2. Arrange the spinach on top of the cabbage, and steam for an additional 3 minutes. Drain in a colander to remove any excess liquid.

3. Put the cabbage and spinach into a warm serving dish. Stir in the butter, lemon zest, and cilantro, mixing well.

4. Sprinkle with salt and pepper and serve immediately.

Pear & Caramel Crisp

SERVES 4
Prepares in 25–30 minutes
Cooks in 45–55 minutes

1 tablespoon unsalted butter,
plus extra for greasing
4 large pears
ice cream, to serve

Crumb Topping

1 cup all-purpose flour
1 teaspoon baking powder
1 stick unsalted butter, diced
⅓ cup packed light brown sugar
2 tablespoons chopped hazelnuts

Caramel

3 tablespoons light corn syrup
3 tablespoons light brown sugar
1 tablespoon unsalted butter
2 tablespoons light cream
½ teaspoon vanilla extract

1. Preheat the oven to 400°F. Lightly grease an ovenproof dish.

2. To make the crumb topping, put the flour and baking powder into a large mixing bowl, then use your fingertips to rub in the unsalted butter until crumbly. Stir in ¼ cup of the sugar and the chopped hazelnuts. Set aside.

3. To make the caramel, put the light corn syrup into a small saucepan over low heat. Add the sugar, unsalted butter, cream, and vanilla extract and bring slowly to a boil. Gently simmer for 3 minutes, stirring constantly, then remove from the heat and set aside.

4. Put the unsalted butter in a skillet and melt over low heat. Meanwhile, peel, core, and coarsely chop the pears, then add them to the pan and cook, stirring gently, for 3 minutes. Stir in the caramel and continue to cook, stirring, over low heat for another 3 minutes.

5. Transfer the pear-and-caramel mixture to the prepared ovenproof dish. Arrange the topping evenly over the top, then sprinkle with the remaining sugar. Bake in the preheated oven for 25–30 minutes, or until the crumb topping is golden brown.

6. Serve immediately with ice cream.

Apple Pie

SERVES 6

Prepares in 45 minutes, plus chilling

Cooks in 50 minutes

Pastry Dough

2¾ cups all-purpose flour, plus extra for dusting

pinch of salt

6 tablespoons butter, diced

⅓ cup vegetable shortening, diced

⅓ cup cold water

beaten egg or milk, for glazing

Filling

5–6 cooking apples (1½–2¼ pounds), such as Granny Smiths, peeled, cored, and sliced

⅔ cup sugar, plus extra for sprinkling

½ –1 teaspoon ground cinnamon, mixed spice or ground ginger

1. To make the dough, sift the flour and salt into a bowl. Add the butter and shortening and rub in with your fingertips until it resembles fine bread crumbs. Add the water and gather together into a dough. Wrap in plastic wrap and chill for 30 minutes.

2. Preheat the oven to 425°F. Roll out almost two-thirds of the dough thinly on a lightly floured surface and use to line a deep 9-inch pie plate.

3. Put the apple slices, sugar, and spice into a bowl and mix thoroughly. Pack the apple mixture into the pastry shell; the filling can come up above the rim. Add 1–2 tablespoons of water, if needed.

4. Roll out the remaining dough on a lightly floured surface to form a lid. Dampen the edges of the pie rim with water and position the lid, pressing the edges firmly together. Trim and crimp the edges. Use the scraps to cut out leaves or other shapes to decorate the top of the pie. Dampen and attach. Glaze the top of the pie with beaten egg, make 1–2 slits in the top, and place the pie plate on a baking sheet.

5. Bake in the preheated oven for 20 minutes, then reduce to 350°F and bake for an additional 30 minutes, or until the pastry is a light golden brown. Serve hot or cold, sprinkled with sugar.

Maple & Pecan Pie

SERVES 8

Prepares in 30–35 minutes, plus chilling and cooling

Cooks in 55 minutes– 1 hour 5 minutes

Pastry Dough

1⅓ cups all-purpose flour, plus extra for dusting

6 tablespoons butter, diced

1 tablespoon superfine sugar

1 egg, beaten with 1 tablespoon cold water

Filling

6 tablespoons butter

⅓ cup packed light brown sugar

⅔ cup maple syrup

⅓ cup light corn syrup

3 extra-large eggs, beaten

1 teaspoon vanilla extract

2 cups pecans

1. To make the dough, sift the flour into a mixing bowl and add the butter. Rub the butter into the flour until the mixture resembles fine bread crumbs. Stir in the superfine sugar and egg-and-water mixture and mix to a firm dough.

2. Turn out the dough onto a lightly floured work surface and lightly knead until smooth. Roll out and use to line a 9½-inch loose-bottom tart pan. Prick the dough all over with a fork and chill in the refrigerator for 30 minutes. Meanwhile, preheat the oven to 400°F.

3. Place the pan on a baking sheet and line with parchment paper and pie weights or dried beans. Bake in the preheated oven for 10 minutes, then remove the paper and weights and bake for an additional 5 minutes, or until the pastry is light golden. Reduce the oven temperature to 350°F.

4. To make the filling, put the butter, brown sugar, maple syrup, and light corn syrup into a saucepan and heat over low heat until melted. Let cool for 5 minutes, then beat in the eggs and vanilla extract. Chop half of the pecans and stir into the mixture.

5. Pour the mixture into the pastry shell and sprinkle with the remaining nuts. Bake in the preheated oven for 35–45 minutes, or until the filling is just set. Serve warm or cold.

Brownie Sundae

SERVES 6

Prepares in 25–30 minutes, plus cooling

Cooks in 45–55 minutes

6 ounces semisweet chocolate, broken into pieces

1½ sticks butter, plus extra for greasing

⅔ cup packed light brown sugar

3 eggs, beaten

1 cup all-purpose flour

1 teaspoon baking powder

Chocolate Fudge Sauce

2 ounces semisweet chocolate, broken into pieces

¼ cup packed light brown sugar

4 tablespoons unsalted butter

3 tablespoons milk

6 scoops vanilla ice cream

1 tablespoon pecans, chopped

6 fresh or maraschino cherries

1. Preheat the oven to 350°F. Grease an 8-inch square cake pan and line the pan with parchment paper.

2. For the brownies, put the chocolate and butter into a large heatproof bowl set over a saucepan of simmering water and heat until melted. Cool for 5 minutes, then whisk in the sugar and eggs. Sift over the flour and baking powder and fold in.

3. Pour the batter into the prepared cake pan and bake in the preheated oven for 35–40 minutes, or until risen and firm to the touch. Let cool in the pan for 15 minutes, then turn out onto a wire rack to cool completely.

4. For the sauce, put all the ingredients into a saucepan and heat gently, stirring all the time, until melted. Bring to a boil and simmer for 1 minute. Remove from the heat and let cool.

5. To serve, cut the brownies into six pieces. Place each piece on a serving plate and top with a large scoop of ice cream. Spoon with the warm sauce and decorate with chopped pecans and cherries.

Weekend Beautiful Breads

Now's the time to show off your baking skills and to enjoy mastering some new bread recipes, from simple, rustic loaves to more sophisticated speciality doughs. The craft of baking bread is centuries old, and it is still a hugely popular weekend pursuit today. By combining a few basic ingredients, you'll be amazed at the tempting range of breads you can create at home.

In this chapter, we include a small but select bunch of beautiful breads and rolls, which will grant you a great way to widen your baking repertoire, showcase your dexterity in baking, and try your hand at creating some tempting now broads to savor and share with family and friends.

Once you have mastered these home baking recipes, you'll be eager to improve your culinary skills and try other techniques, too.

Making bread is relaxing and enjoyable as well as being rewarding (and tasty, too), so what better way to spend part of your weekend, than by creating and baking some delicious bread to share with family and friends? After all, who can resist the enticing, rich aromas of a freshly baked homemade loaf wafting from the kitchen, not to mention the fabulous flavor and crunch to come?

If you have plenty of time on hand, then creating these breads by hand will be most enjoyable. Kneading dough is an excellent way to relax and unwind and can be therapeutic, too, as you work the ingredients together to create a smooth and elastic dough. Bread machines offer an alternative way to make bread for those with less time on their hands, but because it's the weekend, and you'll hopefully have more time to spare, we concentrate our efforts on handmade breads in this chapter.

You can make such a range of recipes—leavened or unleavened flat breads (naan, focaccia, pita bread, chapattis, parathas, roti, tortillas, crispbreads, and so on), quick breads (soda bread, biscuits, muffins, tea breads) and gluten-free breads are just a few of the alternative types of bread you can make at home. So, let's get you started on this hand-picked selection of scrumptious loaves, all of which are perfect for weekend baking and sharing with others.

Popular seeded loaves include the tasty Five-Seed Loaf or, for a flavor-packed loaf with a healthy twist, why not try the Malted Wheat Loaf, which is slightly sweetened with honey? There is also the Crusty Country-Style Loaf, a white traditional loaf lightly dusted with flour that is delicious with butter or lightly toasted. For those who like more of a challenge, the French Baguette could be the one for you—its superb flavor and texture will reward all your patience and proficiency in making it, and it's great with cheese and wine.

Finally, to complete our collection, for those of you who enjoy experimenting with different flours, Spelt Rolls with Spiced Fig Conserve will be the perfect challenge—this recipe not only provides the wholesome bread rolls, it also includes a tasty conserve recipe to accompany them.

Spelt Rolls with Spiced Fig Conserve

For those of you who like experimenting with different flours, prove your baking prowess with these special seeded spelt rolls. Make the scrumptious spiced fig conserve to accompany and your weekend breakfast is done.

MAKES 16 ROLLS AND 1 (16-OUNCE) JAR CONSERVE
Prepares in 45–50 minutes, plus rising, cooling, and chilling
Cooks in 45 minutes

4½ cups whole-wheat spelt flour, plus extra for dusting
1 tablespoon packed dark brown sugar
1 teaspoon sea salt
2 teaspoons active dry yeast
2 tablespoons each sesame seeds, sunflower seeds, and flaxseed, plus extra of each to sprinkle
2 tablespoons virgin olive oil, plus extra to grease
1¼–1½ cups warm water

1 teaspoon milk, to glaze
unsalted butter, to serve

Spiced Fig Conserve

1 cup diced dried figs
3 small crisp, sweet apples, such as Pippin, cored and diced
finely grated zest and juice of 1 orange
1 tablespoon packed light brown sugar
¼ teaspoon ground allspice
1 cup water

1. Put the flour, dark brown sugar, and salt into a bowl and mix well. Stir in the yeast, sesame seeds, sunflower seeds, and flaxseed. Add the oil, then gradually mix in enough warm water to create a soft dough, at first using a wooden spoon, then squeezing together with your hands.

2. Dust a surface with spelt flour, then knead the dough for 5 minutes. Return it to the bowl, cover with lightly oiled plastic wrap, and let rise overnight in the refrigerator.

3. Meanwhile, to make the spiced fig conserve, put the dried figs, apples, orange zest and juice, light brown sugar, allspice, and water into a saucepan. Cover and simmer over medium heat, stirring from time to time, for 30 minutes, or until thick. Let cool. Sterilize a 16-ounce jar, then spoon in the conserve and let stand until completely cold.

Chill in the refrigerator, where it will keep for up to ten days.

4. Line two baking sheets with parchment paper. Dust a work surface with more of the spelt flour. Knead the dough briefly, then cut it into 16 pieces. Roll each piece into a ball, put one ball in the center of each baking sheet, then arrange the others around it, leaving a little space between them.

5. Cover each sheet with lightly oiled plastic wrap and let rise in a warm place for 40–50 minutes. Preheat the oven to 425°F. Remove the plastic wrap, brush the rolls with the milk, and sprinkle with the remaining seeds. Bake in the preheated oven for 15 minutes, or until the rolls are browned and sound hollow when tapped underneath. Serve with butter and the conserve.

Crusty Country-Style Loaf

This traditional crusty loaf is ideal for breakfast or as a midmorning treat—it's great when served thickly sliced, toasted if desired, and loaded with butter and marmalade.

MAKES 1 LOAF
Prepares in 20 minutes,
 plus rising and cooling
Cooks in 40–45 minutes

4¾ cups white bread flour,
 plus extra for dusting
2 teaspoons salt
2 teaspoons active dry yeast
2 tablespoons butter, chilled and diced,
 plus extra for greasing
1 teaspoon superfine sugar
1¾ cups warm water
oil, for greasing

Glaze
1 tablespoon beaten egg
2 teaspoons milk

1. Lightly grease a large baking sheet. Mix the flour, salt, and yeast in a large bowl. Add the butter and rub in to make fine bread crumbs. Stir in the sugar.

2. Make a well in the center of the flour mixture and pour in the warm water. Mix with a knife to make a soft, sticky dough.

3. Turn the dough onto a floured surface and knead for 10 minutes, until smooth and elastic. Shape into a long oval loaf and place on the prepared baking sheet. Slash the top of the loaf six to seven times with a sharp knife. Cover loosely with lightly oiled plastic wrap and let rise in a warm place for 45–55 minutes, until doubled in size. Preheat the oven to 450°F.

4. To make the glaze, beat together the egg and milk with a fork. Lightly brush the glaze all over the loaf.

5. Bake the loaf in the preheated oven for 10 minutes. Reduce the oven temperature to 400°F and bake for an additional 30–35 minutes, or until the loaf is golden and the bottom sounds hollow when tapped with your knuckles. Transfer to a wire rack to cool. Dust lightly with flour before serving.

Malted Wheat Loaf

This wholesome multigrain loaf
has a lovely nutty texture and
flavor. Naturally sweetened
with honey, it tastes great when
spread with cream cheese or
when toasted and buttered.

MAKES 1 LOAF
Prepares in 20 minutes,
 plus rising and cooling
Cooks in 30–35 minutes

2½ cups white bread flour,
 plus extra for dusting
⅔ cup whole-wheat bread flour
⅔ cup malted wheat flakes
3 tablespoons malt powder
1½ teaspoons salt
2 teaspoons active dry yeast
2 teaspoons sunflower seeds
1 tablespoon sunflower oil,
 plus extra for greasing
1 teaspoon honey
1¼ cups warm water

1. Mix together the white flour,
whole-wheat flour, wheat flakes,
malt powder, salt, yeast, and
sunflower seeds in a large bowl
and make a well in the center.

2. Mix together the oil, honey, and
warm water and pour into the bowl.
Mix everything together with a
knife to make a soft, sticky dough.

3. Turn the dough onto a floured
surface and knead for 10 minutes
until smooth and elastic, adding a
little more flour if the dough
becomes too sticky.

4. Place in a bowl, cover with lightly
oiled plastic wrap, and let rise
in a warm place for 1–1½ hours,
or until doubled in size. Preheat
the oven to 425°F. Lightly grease
a 9 x 5 x 3-inch loaf pan.

5. Turn the dough onto a floured
surface and knead again lightly for
1 minute. Shape into an oblong and
place in the loaf pan. Cover with a
clean damp dish towel and let rise in
a warm place for about 30 minutes,
or until the dough has risen above
the top of the edges of the pan.

6. Dust the top of the loaf lightly with
flour. Bake in the preheated oven for
30–35 minutes, or until golden and
the loaf sounds hollow when tapped
on the bottom with your knuckles.
Transfer to a wire rack to cool.

French Baguettes

This classic French loaf is delicious with a range of cheeses and always goes well with a cup of coffee in the morning. The gluten-rich flour creates the coarse, uneven holes inside the loaf.

MAKES 4
Prepares in 20 minutes,
   plus rising and cooling
Cooks in 20–25 minutes

3⅔ cups white bread flour,
   plus extra for dusting
2 teaspoons sugar
2 teaspoons salt
1¾ teaspoons active dry yeast
1½ cups lukewarm water

1. Mix together the flour, sugar, and salt in a bowl. Make a well in the center and add the yeast. Pour the water into the well and mix in the yeast and flour to make a smooth dough.

2. Divide the dough into four pieces and place on a baking sheet. Cover with plastic wrap and let rise for 30 minutes.

3. Transfer the dough pieces to a surface lightly dusted with flour, punch down, and shape each piece into a long 2-inch-thick roll.

4. Place the uncooked baguettes on a dish towel dusted with flour. Make folds in the towel to separate each baguette from the next. It is important that the loaves are not too close together so that they have room to rise. Cover with plastic wrap and let rise in a warm place for about 30 minutes.

5. Preheat the oven to 475°F and place a bowl of water in the bottom of the oven. Line a baking sheet with parchment paper. Place the baguettes on the prepared sheet and use a sharp knife to make five diagonal cuts in each.

6. Dust the baguettes with flour and bake in the preheated oven for 20–25 minutes, or until golden and the bottoms sound hollow when tapped underneath. Transfer to a wire rack to cool.

Five-Seed Loaf

Mixed seeds add delicious flavor, texture, and crunch to this popular loaf. Serve it freshly baked and spread with butter for breakfast, brunch, or lunch and any guests will devour this crusty bread in no time at all.

MAKES 1 LOAF
Prepares in 25 minutes,
  plus rising and cooling
Cooks in 25–30 minutes

2 cups whole-wheat bread flour,
  plus extra for dusting
1⅔ cups white bread flour
1 teaspoon salt
¾ cup five-seed mix
  (including sesame, pumpkin,
  sunflower, hemp, and flaxseed)
2¼ teaspoons active dry yeast
1 tablespoon packed light brown sugar
2 tablespoons sunflower oil,
  plus extra for greasing
1¼ cups lukewarm water

1. Lightly grease a baking sheet with oil.

2. Mix the whole-wheat flour, white flour, salt, seed mix, and yeast in a large bowl. Stir in the sugar.

3. Mix together the oil and water to combine. Make a well in the center of the flour mixture and pour in the liquid. Mix thoroughly with a knife to make a soft sticky dough.

4. Turn out the dough onto a lightly floured work surface and knead for 5–7 minutes, or until smooth and elastic. Shape the dough into a round ball and place on the prepared baking sheet.

5. Dust the top of the loaf with whole-wheat flour and let rest in a warm place for 1–1½ hours, or until doubled in size.

6. Meanwhile, preheat the oven to 425°F. Bake the loaf in the preheated oven for 5 minutes. Reduce the oven temperature to 400°F and bake for an additional 20–25 minutes, or until golden and the bottom sounds hollow when tapped with your knuckles.

7. Transfer to a wire rack to cool completely.

Monday Morning Boosters

With your batteries sufficiently recharged, you'll be feeling refreshed, revitalized, and ready to face the working week ahead. However, many of us are all too familiar with that sinking Monday morning feeling, but fear not as we try to make Monday morning as bearable as possible. We feature a mouthwatering selection of supercharged juices, energy cookies, and power snacks, guaranteed to get you off on the right foot.

It's important to try to start the week with a positive mindset, because it will set the stage for the week ahead. If you can get up early and exercise first thing, it is a great way to get your circulation going and put you in the right mood for the rest of the day

A healthy breakfast is important, because it gives you vital energy and gets your day off to a good start, as well as improving performance and concentration. However, if breakfast just isn't your thing or you have limited time before you set off on your commute to work, then one of these energy boosters is a great way to keep the stomach growls at bay and nourish the body.

If you have a juicer, citrus press, or blender, it will come into its own if you need a quick energy boost to get you going in the morning. Nutritious and delicious juices and smoothies are fast and easy to make and will set you up for the day ahead, so it's worth investing in a suitable piece of equipment if this is your thing.

There is a wide variety of juicers and citrus presses available, ranging in quality, efficiency, and price, from simple, straightforward juicers or juice extractors to more serious, stylish, sophisticated appliances. The same goes for a blender, which will also prove to be a really useful gadget to have when making other recipes, such as soups, sauces, and so on.

Freshly squeezed juices (and some smoothies too) are tasty and nutritious, because they are loaded with fruit and vegetables, delivering a bounty of vitamins and minerals and providing an easy way to drink some of your recommended daily intake of these nutrients.

So, if you need some great ideas for quick and easy juices to wake you up in the morning, then look no farther. We include the aptly named and delicious Dandelion Sunrise Smoothie or tantalizing Turbo Recharge Smoothie, but if you simply need some pepping up, then the refreshing Mint Rejuvenating Juice will revitalize you in no time at all.

Alternatively, when you don't have the luxury of time on your side, the Chocolate & Peanut Butter Energy Balls can be prepared ahead and will supply a much-needed energizer first thing. The Ginger & Oat No-Bake Cookies will also provide an ideal on-the-run power snack if you are short of time, or if you need the perfect pick-me-up a little later on to keep you on the ball.

Dandelion Sunrise Smoothie

SERVES 1
Prepares in 10 minutes
No cooking

½ cup dandelion greens
1 cup curly green kale
1 cup chilled water
¼ cup cashew nuts
1½ teaspoons coconut butter
1 tablespoon sunflower seeds

1. Put the dandelion greens, kale, and water into a blender and blend until smooth.

2. Add the cashew nuts, coconut butter, and sunflower seeds and blend again until the mixture is smooth and creamy.

3. Pour into a glass and serve immediately.

Turbo Recharge Smoothie

SERVES 1
Prepares in 15–20 minutes
No cooking

½ honeydew melon, seeded and coarsely chopped
1 banana, coarsely chopped
1 kiwi, coarsely chopped
¾ cup green seedless grapes
small handful of watercress
½ cup unsweetened rice, almond, or soy milk
small handful of crushed ice (optional)

1. Put the melon, banana, kiwi, grapes, and watercress into a blender and blend until smooth.

2. Add the milk and crushed ice, if using, to the blender and blend again, until smooth.

3. Pour into a glass and serve immediately.

Mint Rejuvenating Juice

SERVES 1
Prepares in 15 minutes
No cooking

½ Galia or honeydew melon,
thickly sliced
3 cups baby spinach
2 sprigs fresh flat-leaf parsley
3 large stems fresh mint
small handful of ice (optional)

1. Feed the melon, spinach, parsley, and two stems of mint through a juicer.

2. Fill a glass halfway with ice, if using, then pour in the juice.

3. Garnish with the remaining stem of mint and serve immediately.

Ginger & Oat No-Bake Cookies

MAKES 8

Prepares in 10–15 minutes,
plus chilling

Cooks in 8–10 minutes

4 tablespoons unsalted butter

1 cup heavy cream

1 heaping tablespoon unsweetened,
smooth peanut butter

3 tablespoons honey

1 tablespoon ground ginger

2⅓ cups rolled oats

1. Put the butter, cream, and peanut butter into a small saucepan. Bring to a boil over medium heat, stirring occasionally from time to time. Turn the heat down to medium–low and cook for 5 minutes.

2. Put all the remaining ingredients into the pan and stir to mix well.

3. Line a baking sheet with parchment paper. Drop tablespoons of the dough onto the baking sheet, then cover and chill in the refrigerator for 25 minutes to harden before serving.

Chocolate & Peanut Butter Energy Balls

When your energy levels are low, these tempting energy balls will provide the perfect pick-me-up. They can easily be prepared ahead, so are ideal for those short of time but in need of a quick energizer first thing.

MAKES 8
Prepares in 20 minutes,
  plus chilling
No cooking

½ cup blanched almonds
¼ cup unsweetened peanut butter
2 tablespoons coarsely chopped
  unsalted peanuts
3 tablespoons flaxseed

1 ounce bittersweet chocolate,
  finely chopped
pinch of salt
1 teaspoon unsweetened cocoa powder

1. Put the almonds into a food processor and process for a minute, until you have the texture of coarse flour.

2. Put the peanut butter, peanuts, flaxseed, chocolate, and a small pinch of salt into a large bowl and mix to combine. Add the almond flour, reserving 1½ tablespoons of the flour. Mix until you have a texture resembling chunky clay.

3. Sprinkle the remaining almond flour and the cocoa powder onto a plate and mix with a teaspoon.

4. Form a tablespoon-size blob of the peanut mixture into a ball, forming it between the palms of your hands. Roll it in the cocoa powder mixture, then transfer to a plate. Make an additional seven balls in the same way.

5. Cover with plastic wrap and chill the balls in the refrigerator for at least 30 minutes before serving, or they can be stored for up to two days.

Index